AF279203

HOSANNA
By Deborah Santana

Songs of praise to the rising sun,

Like tips of fire, radiating prayers are sculpted

in calm devotion,

chanted from the center of my heart's wall.

Impermanent like the rising edge of the sky,

my yearnings reach into the shimmering

robes of sacred meditation.

Mine is a long journey of breath to sky,

spinning prayer wheels in faithful flight.

I am endeared to the silence,

to the surprise of wisdoms that return on rays of light.

I am one among thousands and thousands seeking a meaningful life.

Like morning's first finches waking to sing,

Love, compassion, and peace take wing

As the sun breathes us open.

"I was not able to stop reading *Loving the Fire*. Not only to follow Deborah's journey—especially her childhood, her parents, and her deep care for her own children—but her own growth, her support in helping spread the truth and heritage of Black people. I love this book on so many levels. So glad Deborah Santana became a writer."

—NATALIE GOLDBERG
Author of Writing on Empty and Writing Down the Bones

"*Loving the Fire* takes us on a journey of self-discovery, compassion, and courage. Deborah Santana, once a student and now a teacher in her own right, embodies the healing power of empathy and intuition. Her journey inspires us all to live with purpose, curiosity, and gratitude."

—JUDITH ORLOFF
MD, New York Times Bestselling Author of The Empath's Survival Guide

"Deborah Santana's quiet demeanor is camouflage for the courageous, warrior woman she truly is. With sound introspection, and a candidly honest examination of herself, she takes us on a grand and entertaining journey into finding, embracing, and accepting the person God purposed her to be on earth. A most rewarding follow up to her memoir *Space Between the Stars*."

—LATANYA RICHARDSON JACKSON
Actress, Director, Producer

"Deborah Santana's luminous new memoir *Loving The Fire: Choosing Me, Finding Freedom*, is a fiercely courageous declaration of selfhood. Told with grace, humility and unflinching candor, Santana takes us on a journey, from her humble beginnings in Louisiana to Northern California, across the ocean to the motherland and back again. Every chapter offers a window into the pivotal moments, encounters, connections, and lessons that forged her. How Santana has lived so fully is a wonder and an inspiration. This book is a gift to be cherished and shared."

—NATALIE BASZILE
Author of Queen Sugar and We Are Each Other's Harvest

"Like a breath of fresh air, *Loving the Fire* is beautiful, light-filled, and intimate. Deborah Santana traces her journey from her deep multicultural roots in the American South and West to the hidden costs of a life lived in proximity to stardom. Coming into her deeper self, she guides readers on a soulful passage through Mexico, Africa, and postcolonial feminist thought. Santana paints in words a deeply spiritual and uplifting family album that illuminates the value of courage—of seeking and following one's heart—despite outward pressure to conform and settle. Refreshing and nourishing, this memoir is a treatise on how to access one's inner power. It is as restorative as a glass of cool water to the parched."

—THOMAS ALLEN HARRIS
Filmmaker, Professor in the Practice of Yale University Film and Media Studies & Black Studies, and Co-Director of the Family Pictures Institute for Inclusive Storytelling

LOVING THE FIRE

Choosing Me, Finding Freedom

DEBORAH SANTANA

Broad Book Press and Studio 33 Books, Publishers

Cover photography by Michael Collopy
Cover and book design by Charles McStravick
Endpapers collage design, *Where I come from, where I stand,* by Deborah Santana

Hardcover ISBN: 978-1963549409
eBook ISBN: 978-1963549416

Published in the United States as a collaboration
between Broad Book Press and Studio 33 Books.

Library of Congress Control Number: 2025924730

This book is printed on post-consumer recycled paper.

For my parents, Jo Frances and Saunders King,
and my sister Kitsaun King.

For all the women who run through fire.

For the future, my children Salvador, Stella,
and Angelica Faith.

With gratitude . . .

CONTENTS

Prologue ix

Introduction xi

1. THE ORIGINS OF MY FAMILY TREE 1

2. WE WERE KINGS 11

3. THE ALCHEMY OF LIFE 29

4. MoAD DREAMS 37

5. A MORE RADIANT FORM 43

6. THE STUNNING MYSTERIES OF LIFE 53

7. ARTISTS FOR A NEW SOUTH AFRICA 59

8. CROSSING THE ABYSS TO ME 75

9. RESPOND TO EVERYTHING IN LOVE 81

10. GRADUATION 89

11. WALKING THE MOUNTAINS 103

12. THE GIRLS OF DARAJA 107

13. TRUTH IS EVERYWHERE 123

14. RUMI AWAKENING 131

15. UNSUNG HEROES OF COMPASSION 135

16. DANCING ON THE WAY 141

17. ALL THE WOMEN IN MY FAMILY SING 149

18. CEREMONY 155

19. CENTRAL TO THE AMERICAN STORY 161

20. THE WOMEN'S MARCH 167

21. INCOMPATIBLE SOFTWARE 175

22. TO COURAGE 183

Epilogue 189

How to Walk Through Fire 191

Acknowledgments 193

About the Author 194

PROLOGUE

It was New Year's Eve 2006. Three votive candles flickered before me, their light soft against a velvet-black sky outside the window. I asked myself the questions that had been echoing for years: Am I happy? Can I live in my own reality? Do I have the courage to break the contract I made at twenty-two—to step into my autonomy and thrive outside of my marriage?

For thirty-four years, my identity was entwined with a man the world knew well—but few knew the woman behind the scenes. For the last thirteen of those years, I pleaded for closeness, for the tearing back of our protective skins to bare our true natures. But the intimacy I longed for remained just out of reach. I had hidden myself behind a self-imposed mask of composure, a "Mona Lisa smile" that concealed my pain and diminished my truth.

That night, in the stillness before the new year, my heart spoke clearly: I would rather be alone than continue to compromise my soul. An inner voice whispered: It is time to let Carlos be who he is in this incarnation— and for me to seek God, ecstasy, and divine love on my own.

Through tears and smiles, I began the shedding. I had been the vice president and chief operating officer of Santana Management, raising three children, managing our foundation, and serving others—but now, my work was to be true to my own spirit. I was discovering the woman beneath the roles, the one who no longer needed to hide her light or filter her existence through another's gaze.

Almost twenty years have passed since that moment, and I know that nothing is permanent—not love nor grief, not joy nor sorrow. Everything ends; everything begins anew. This is the story of that ending—and of the beginning that followed.

INTRODUCTION

At the outset, I must warn readers that I am a positive person, consumed with faith that all is going along according to a divine plan, believing my soul comes from the great Soul. At times, I have been disillusioned with my circumstances and experienced trials by fire. My faith in God has held me close and guided me through these times. I imagine this is influenced by my soul's pre-birth intention (karma) as well as the name my mother chose for me.

I was named for St. Deborah the Prophetess, and even though I didn't understand the power of this woman until I was an adult, her essence is within me. According to the Bible, St. Deborah was a courageous military leader who defended the Israelites against the Canaanites who had oppressed them for twenty years. Her leadership is recorded in the Old Testament's "Song of Deborah." My mother read the Bible daily, and her faith deepened in the recounting of Biblical characters' troubles and triumphs. She was also a pacifist. I believe she chose the name Deborah for me because of St. Deborah's strength to fight against injustice and her closeness to God.

By naming me "Deborah," my mother allowed me to believe that women can be powerful leaders, slay enemies, and change systems that oppress others. I am fortunate to have had mentors who gave me words and actions to follow.

I came to understand my life through my Black ancestors' personal stories, the ones left out of history books and often missing from census accounts. It was at the dinner table that my character was formed, listening to how my Black ancestors persevered in a land that didn't honor them. When researching my genealogy, my elders' lives revealed struggles they endured and their love of community, both of which fuel my philanthropic work today.

I am a champion of the marginalized, and those whose voices are silenced. I make choices for my own life by trusting what feels right, and I encourage others to do the same. This memoir is about the choices I've made, the courage I have been gifted to live with, and the consciousness I have grown into that enables me to have compassion for myself and others.

Loving the Fire is about the life I have created since the publication of my first memoir, *Space Between the Stars*. It is about living on my own after admitting that I was dying in my thirty-four-year marriage to Carlos Santana and how earth-shattering the decision was for me to leave, yet I left so that I could live free. I will tell you how Spirit guided me through that time and unfolded the person I am today.

My wish is that this account of my life's excursions inspires you to reach for all that is possible in your life and to love the being that you are. In the Indigenous tradition, I believe every sentient being is alive with Spirit's essence, which can teach us how to breathe, even in the most painful times, and engage in this extraordinary, spectacular, stunning human adventure with wonder.

bell hooks' words align with this belief:

> *"Spiritual life is first and foremost about commitment*
> *to a way of thinking and behaving that honors*
> *principles of inter-being and interconnectedness.*
> *When I speak of the spiritual, I refer to the recognition*
> *within everyone that there is a place of mystery in our lives*
> *where forces that are beyond human desire or will*

alter circumstances and/or guide and direct us.
I call these forces 'Divine Spirit.'"

(bell hooks, *All About Love: New Visions*)

Each day is ripe for experiencing the full range of human emotions and Divine miracles.

Each moment can be a step toward a holy evolution.

THE ORIGINS OF
MY FAMILY TREE

This is what I can tell you: My grandmother was bulletproof.

You might think I am speaking metaphorically, but I mean it as literal truth: She survived a gunshot wound and didn't let it stop her from continuing her mission, which was to bring the Gospel to heal people's souls. When I draw upon my strength, I draw from my ancestors—a tradition of women whose appearances gave no indication of their inner sturdiness, their sense of being warriors. Everything I am comes from this cloth.

When I have momentarily lost myself or found myself disappearing in someone else's shadow, it is my grandmother's memory that shakes me awake again. *Stand tall,* I remind myself. *Like the women who came before you.*

Not that Grandmother was tall in stature. That's the metaphorical part. When she finished growing in adolescence, Sarah Anasilistine Mitchell stretched to a mere five foot one. Her pecan-hued skin, long straight black hair, and carved cheekbones hinted of her Choctaw, Cherokee, and Adai Caddo Indian lineage. Born May 6, 1878, in Sabine, Louisiana, she was reared on a farm with her ten brothers and sisters. Sarah was the oldest of this brood, and I imagine her herding her seven sisters and two brothers (one sister died at two weeks old) from their small wooden house to play in the mangroves, running away from brown snakes and capturing small tree frogs.

Sarah attended school through ninth grade and was baptized in the Houston River northeast of Starks, at the mouth of Bear Head Creek in Calcasieu Parish. The gum and pine trees gave off a spicy scent, a fragrance she would always identify with her ceremonious acceptance into the church. Her parents were Methodists, and her roots were biracial, common for the times.

My grandfather, Judge L. King, was born in Alexandria, Louisiana, on July 19, 1872. With dark eyes that sent forth a princely strength, he stood five foot eleven with a broad chest and curly black hair parted on the left side. In 1897, he saw Sarah in Sabine's general store while she purchased flour, yams, and dried beans for her mother. Striding slowly to the end of the counter, he introduced himself, and a year later, they were betrothed in Orange, Texas, thirty-three miles west of Calcasieu Parish. They moved to Lake Charles, Louisiana, and began their family, eventually having five children: Jay, Judge, Ulysses, Daisy, and Saunders, who was my father.

Grandfather Judge was a chore laborer who traveled with his father, Thomas Jefferson (Tom) King, to Texas and throughout Louisiana, staying in boarding houses while earning money from local jobs to take back home. Judge eventually settled on work in sawmills, where, as a Black laborer, his pay was low, often in cash, and year-round. He worked as a block setter, riding on the carriage that transported logs to the main saw, which meant that he squared up the first two edges of the log and took the controls to choose the milling cuts. The job required exacting skills to determine the calculations needed for the thickness of the lumber to minimize waste. Sawmills were dangerous workplaces by nature of the whirring belts and pulleys, planer mill, and band saws. Mills were also vulnerable to fires.

From 1900 to 1920, Louisiana was one of the country's top three lumber-producing states, with millions of dollars invested in lumber manufacturing facilities that provided employment for Blacks and whites.

Because Grandfather worked steadily, Grandmother Sarah did not worry about what they did not have; the children were provided for and well fed. When he traveled to distant towns to labor in other mills, however, Grandfather was tense amid the sanctioned violence toward African-American men and women by the Ku Klux Klan and the Jim Crow laws that forced Blacks to enter establishments through back doorways and drink from separate water fountains.

Groups of white missionaries from England and the West Coast of America came to Lake Charles and traveled into Lafayette and Crowley, preaching the Gospel of Jesus Christ to "save" sinners. During the day, they fanned out into the fields to proselytize and at night slipped surreptitiously into family homes teaching a theology of holiness and anointing by the Holy Spirit. Many local people wanted the promised blessings and justification in the sight of God and welcomed missionaries to read Scriptures with them.

Grandmother felt a strong calling to follow the Holiness teachings and was converted to the sanctified beliefs and baptized in the Holy Ghost. She received the gift of speaking in tongues, or glossolalia, the phenomenon of being caught up in Spirit and hearing a message in a language unrecognizable to most but able to be interpreted by an anointed believer.

She began preaching in the Methodist Church before my grandfather had faith. Judge told Sarah, *"Keep going to church and pray for me, but don't take the children. They can stay here with me."* After one year, Grandfather had a conversion experience at work. He had worn a pistol for years to protect himself, and one day he heard God tell him, *"Pull off your gun."* Then God spoke again: *"Pull off your gun."* Grandfather walked to the mill pond and threw the gun in. Spirit filled him, and he raised his arms and began praying in a loud voice, *"Thank you, God. Thank you, God."*

The local sheriff stopped him. *"What's going on, Judge?"*

Grandfather proclaimed, *"I've just been saved."*

After his conversion, Judge and Sarah traveled to other towns in Louisiana—Monroe and Shreveport, and Caddo Parish, a small cotton community, where they preached under a large oak tree at night, telling others about the good news of Jesus Christ.

Grandmother established a school on land that a local business owner gave the community. This was an instance of generosity from neighboring whites, an act that made my grandparents realize that there could be equality even as they worked and lived within a social order of oppression. They did not discredit all members of the white society and welcomed whites in their church. Everyone assisted in raising timber posts and beams and installing windows to build the school. Grandfather continued preaching the Gospel, baptizing believers with water, and giving communion using grape juice and small wafers.

My grandparents built their first church in Keachi, Louisiana. They nailed each sideboard, installed the roof, laid flooring, and set windows and doors in place. Christ Holy Sanctified Church was incorporated in 1910, and it did not establish a hierarchical system of leadership; everyone was "Brother" or "Sister." Grandfather traveled with Brother C.H. Mason and Brother C.P. Jones, preaching and baptizing people in Louisiana, East Texas, and Mississippi.

Growing up, I didn't know that in free Black communities, political leaders were elected to local offices, such as the school board, and Louisiana became the first state in US history to have a Black governor, P.B.S. Pinchback, and lieutenant governor, Oscar Dunn, who was the first Black acting governor in the United States in 1871. Although persecution of Blacks was commonplace, there were some gains in equality that empowered Black citizens. The King family's daily life was strengthened by the stability of Grandmother and Grandfather's faith and the close community life they built.

When my dad, Saunders, was a boy, he often played on the front porch when his father returned from working in the sawmill. He grabbed his father's tin lunch pail to carry inside, hoping his father brought him a treat.

"Dad! What do you have for me?" he asked. Judge often brought a hard candy, a penny, or some token that was grand for a young boy.

"What do you think I have, Sambo?" Grandfather asked, opening his hand to reveal a round sweet.

Shrinking back from the sting of the name his father used, Dad boiled with anger and bad feelings. He had seen minstrel shows where dark-skinned Black men acted silly and docile. He didn't say anything and took the hard candy in his hand. The next time Grandfather called him Sambo, Dad said, *"Please don't use that name, Father. It's bad."*

Gentle understanding softened Grandfather's face. He knew the brutality of the racist words. Grandfather said, *"Why, son, of course I won't."*

Saunders Samuel King was my father's given name, but the negative depiction of Black men as "Sambo," "coon," or other less-than-dignified ethnophaulisms signifying inequality to their white counterparts, caused him to legally change his middle name from Samuel to Steven so he would never be mistakenly called Sambo again.

Another story about my dad's childhood recounted how he did not feel well one Sunday and stayed home from church to rest. He was five. As the church service was letting out and all the "saints" walked outside of the sanctuary, talking to one another, people noticed my grandfather's automobile heading for the church. Jumping up and down, arms pointing at the sight, they shrieked, *"That looks like Saunders!"* They could see the top of his head as he was standing up to reach the foot pedal, turning the steering wheel, and heading their way.

Somehow, Dad knew how to start the car but had no idea how to stop it. Maybe he felt alone in the house, or maybe he just wanted to drive—we didn't know. But a church member averted disaster, running alongside, jumping in, and pulling the handbrake. I never heard of a spanking or any punishment—just the account of a young boy with great imagination and daring.

Like many Black families, the Kings joined the migration West to escape the caste system of the South. They first moved to East Texas and established two new churches, and then in 1918, the family continued to Los Angeles, where they attracted only two church members.

"This is not the place for our church," Judge told Sarah, discouraged but not defeated.

Many former Louisiana residents had relocated to Northern California to work in lumber, and in 1923, Judge and Sarah followed the

Southern transplants to Oroville, assimilating into the Black populace there. Oroville was building a new city hall where men could find work.

Their small church building was near land owned by white ranchers who disapproved of their style of singing, playing tambourines, and praying aloud in the Spirit. One Sunday, a group of men rode by on horses and shot their guns through the windows. The parishioners had seen them before—riding close to the front door, brandishing their guns, and shouting, *"Get out of here, n—gers!"*— but they weren't expecting violence. Screams filled the church. Grandmother was struck by a bullet and fell to the floor clutching her stomach. Congregants ran to her side, kneeling while they lifted their arms to God in prayer. *"Lord, keep this sister. We pray for your mercy."* Moaning and crying, they carried her to a car and to the hospital where the bullet was removed and Grandmother was sent home to recover.

One year later, someone burned the church down in the middle of the night—a continuation of religious persecution and racial prejudice. Judge and Sarah roused the family once again and moved to Oakland. Their family and a cadre of believers built another church, wood plank by wood plank. The labor was something they were accustomed to out of necessity, and they were adept and artful with their hands. My grandparents visited the neighborhood bars, rental apartments, and corner stores to invite everyone to church: the sleeping car porters, seamstresses, nurses, teachers, and sex workers. Everyone was offered foot washing, water baptism, and sacraments of wafers and grape juice. Christ Holy Sanctified Church lived on.

THE MEMORIES AND IMAGES WERE THREE-DIMENSIONAL FOR ME as I looked in my grandparents' eyes in photos and read early church history in our scant family archives. Hearing these experiences recounted, I was gifted a strong backbone. If my ancestors could endure hate crimes and assaults on their mode of worship, I could stand tall in the face of visible and invisible condemnation and attack, too.

I wish my Grandmother King had kept journals. Such stories they would have told. By the time I was born, she was seventy-three years old and had buried my grandfather six years earlier. He had died of pulmonary tuberculosis, his parishioners praying day and night for him to live until he asked them to stop praying and let him go.

I wondered if Grandmother felt bereft and alone when Grandfather died. What did she receive from God that gave her the strength to continue? What were her morning and nightly prayers?

In my early years, our family lived with her, my Aunt Daisy, and her son, Sebastian, in Berkeley. It was a big, rambling house with a row of filmy windows around the bedrooms upstairs. Grandmother's distinctive voice was soft and crackly. We often sat together on the couch in the living room, discussing the events of the moment, her soft, wrinkled hand holding mine. *"Baby,"* she called me. *"Recite your lines from the Christmas play."* I obeyed, watching her lips curve into a smile at my juvenile performance.

The house had a dusty backyard where my sister, Kitsaun, liked to furiously pedal a tricycle with me on the back. One day, she decided to jump off the tricycle and roll onto the dry grass. *"Ta da!"* she exclaimed, thinking her acrobatics were clever. But the tricycle reared up, and the handlebars whacked my chin, and blood spurted out.

Kitsaun ran to me, yelling, *"Oh no!"* She took my hand and dragged me into the house, screaming for Grandmother. I sometimes notice the scar when I look closely at my face in the mirror and fondly remember growing up with a family who loved me.

My mother also named Kitsaun, but unlike my Biblical moniker, Mom created my sister's name from the woman in the hospital bed next to her on the day she gave birth. Kit San was the Japanese woman's name. Mom thought of putting the first and last names together and bring Dad's name in too. Kitsaun has always prided herself on her beautiful, unusual name.

Grandmother eventually moved with Uncle Judge from Berkeley to a farm in Chowchilla, a small agricultural town in Central California. Kitsaun and I stayed with her for a week each blistering hot summer, rising with the roosters, and following Grandmother to feed the chickens each morning. She wore round wire-rimmed glasses that sat heavily on her round brown cheeks, and her fine hair was braided into a bun at her nape. She showed us how to plant seeds and water the tomato plants. "*Kitsoo* (this was what her pronunciation of Kitsaun sounded like to me), *bring Deborah to the garden. I want to show you girls how to pick green beans.*" Kitsaun held my hand and walked me down the cement path beside the garage to the fenced-in rows of vegetables.

My family attended Christ Holy Sanctified Church, a rousing service where we sang, clapped, and swayed to upbeat music that parishioners played on banjos, guitars, piano, and tambourines. We sat in a light oak pew near Aunt Bitsy's piano bench. Her skin, the color of brewed tea with a generous splash of milk, held her beaming eyes as she lifted her hands above the keys, playing chords of "How Great Thou Art" and "We've Come This Far by Faith," her voice enunciating each word, affirming her belief in God. Often, the lyrics of the songs brought worshippers to tears, as their bodies rocked side to side with the melodies, raising their arms and calling out, "*Thank you, Jesus,*" and "*Praise you, Lord.*"

I felt my emotions rise with this Spirit that vibrated throughout the sanctuary. Yet I was never "filled with the Holy Spirit" in the way other believers were—falling to the floor in a semiconscious state—and I didn't mind. Grandmother felt the Spirit and raised her arm, waving it slowly side to side above her head. I mimicked her. The energy of healing love suffused the sanctuary, touching me, and I looked around at the faces of women and men being transformed with light through their devotion to God.

This form of worship was born of the sorrow and persecution of enslavement, the loss of loved ones to lynchings, and beatings on plantations, and was a uniquely African American experiential and emotional expression. The freedom of one's soul occurred in overcoming, but that did not happen when enslavement legally ended. African Americans repeatedly sought freedom because oppression and racism never stopped. In the sermons and songs of my family church, we knew that within every cell there was a restorative spirit from beyond the visible realm.

Grandmother's voice was never loud. Her bubbly laughter and sermons in church were a balm. She was an elder in the church, and hundreds of congregants not only saw her as national vice president but Mother of the church because of her extensive knowledge of the Bible and her preaching about the interrelatedness of heart to Spirit. Grandmother dedicated her life to seeking God and imparted a spiritual awareness to me through her place on the church dais. She cherished listening to my Uncle Ulysses S. King's sermons while sitting in the solid oak pulpit chair. She stayed with Aunt Daisy when she came to Oakland to attend church and be with our family. She prayed aloud before each meal, and her voice was soft when she instructed me, *Say your prayers every night.* I knew those prayers were a covering to my life even then.

I found a booklet she wrote, *Guide Directory of the Women's Home Missionary Society of Christ's Holy Sanctified Church of America Inc.* The chapters covered a range of topics, including: "The Home Mission Society," "By-Laws," "How to Organize," "Pulpit Committee," "On Sewing," "Committee on Good Work," "Order of Business," "State President," and my personal favorite, "Committee on Backsliders." The fourteen-page booklet was not dated; I assume it was published in the 1940s.

Grandmother taught each of her five children to bake cakes on Saturdays. She also insisted they present genteel manners to the world with proper English diction and use no slang. Later, I tried to explain to my own children how rap music and the casual, if not crude, vernacular of young people today was not the way I was raised, but society had different mores and what was of value to me did not resonate with them.

Church was always a time to celebrate the good things in life and to keep the faith that what was not good would be overcome. Many times, in my childhood, I looked around at the adults caught in the spell of Spirit and felt like thunder and lightning were moving through the church, cleansing us.

When Grandmother was one month shy of ninety-four years old, she was visiting Aunt Daisy when God "called her home," as the church community labels dying. She was never ill and never suffered; she just went to sleep after saying her prayers and awakened on the other side of life. I always believed that the gentleness in which she left this earth was a blessing in response to the love she gave everyone. The church and family wept, but in the Christian tradition, we believed we would see her again. Her legacy lives on in the church that still thrives in Oakland, with my cousin Ulysses Stephen King, Jr. as leader.

I am filled with gratitude for the gifts bestowed on me from the lineage of women in my family; my grandmother's and grandfather's African-American roots of strength, endurance, and elegance; and my mother, Jo Frances, and her four sisters—Neomi (Nomi), Juanita (Nita), Ginger (Dini), and Agatha (Aggie)—of Irish, English, and Scottish descent, who imbued me with wild laughter, feminist power, and the love of hard work. Most importantly, all my ancestors gave me the gift of believing in myself.

2

WE WERE KINGS

ONE OF MY FAVORITE PHOTOGRAPHS OF MY PARENTS shows them standing side by side in front of a house with a picket fence. Both have their hands in their pockets—Mom's are inside her unbuttoned coat; Dad's are in his wide-legged pleated wool pants, his plaid shirt open from the waist down. His full lips are parted, white teeth visible. Mom's red-stained lips are open in a wide smile, her eyes looking straight into the camera, hair pulled back in a ponytail. Their stance suggests they are still dating, not yet intimately joined, both beautiful and Mom oh-so-young. They are shoulder to shoulder, touching without embrace.

This was the way they looked out into the world: as one unit, one beloved force—and was how I always saw them. They were revolutionaries in the way they chose to live: free, Black and white, older and younger, my father a musician/songwriter, my mother a feminist government worker. They were visionaries who chafed against America's segregation laws and created a family that was a safe dwelling place for Kitsaun and me. Through their example, we learned to keep our backs straight and our eyes forward, not cowering in the threatening political environment for people of color and our mixed ethnicity.

Our home on Majestic Avenue in San Francisco was in the Ingleside neighborhood, where Black, Hawaiian, Latino, white, and Asian families lived side by side. Mom and Dad owned our two-bedroom home, sometimes struggling to make the mortgage payment but never in danger of losing the edifice that was a castle to us.

We were west of Twin Peaks, on the land of the Ramaytush Ohlone people. A hill was at the top of our cul-de-sac, beckoning neighborhood children to climb the rock formation above the dry grass. The city was often shrouded in fog, but Mom knew how to coax the brief afternoon sunlight onto her plants. She raised pink geraniums and purple-petaled African violets in terra-cotta pots on our kitchen windowsill. She tended to them, watering beneath each leaf at just the right time, gently prying wilted blooms off the stems. Saturdays were chore days when we changed our sheets, swept the front porch, and dusted the living room coffee table and lamps. I was responsible for ironing the pillowcases—the only items Mom trusted me not to burn. Mom trained Kitsaun and me to take care of our bodies, too. *"Wash behind your ears and the skin by your ankles. Dirt collects there,"* Mom said.

She modeled feminism in all she did and taught us to add just enough moxie to poke the system of injustice and stand as fighters for equality. In any conflict, Mom faced down neighbors and storekeepers who spoke harshly to us. Her intrepidness shaped my sister and me.

We typically drove to Grandmother King's farm for summer vacations, but once went to Knott's Berry Farm and Disneyland, staying in a modest motel with a swing and slide beside a small kidney-shaped pool. We had one Samsonite suitcase for us all and brown paper bags packed with homemade bologna sandwiches for the drive. I always brought a book to read in the car as Dad drove us through the middle of the state, with the radio playing soft jazz or a Giants baseball game broadcast from windy Candlestick Park.

We traveled well together, our parents sending a glare to the back seat if any bickering started. Dad often pulled off the highway to find parks or creeks where we could rest. Kitsaun and I held hands and walked behind Mom to dip our feet in shallow water while Dad relaxed under a tree.

We could hear Dad's mellifluous whistle through the air, his lips pursed, never taking a breath as melodies floated like birdsong. Dad whistled a lot: standing at the stove frying hamburgers (the only dinner I remember him fixing), when picking us up from school, and while walking down city streets. Dad learned to whistle as a kid, and whenever I heard it, it calmed me, like his five-foot-eleven height that towered over me and made me lift my head high.

Our kitchen had a long wooden table where we came together for family dinners. Kitsaun and I set the table with quilted placemats and thin-handled flatware with an etched pattern of a flower vine. The galley kitchen was on the other side of tall cupboards, and we carried our plates of cooked food around the painted wall. Sometimes Kitsaun reached her foot out to trip me as I walked by. Mom would snap, *"Kitsaun! Stop causing trouble,"* and Kitsaun would slink away. We congregated on the couch after dinner, Dad playing 33 RPM albums of Duke Ellington, Billie Holiday, Wes Montgomery, and Dinah Washington while he strummed his Gibson guitar.

Mom's basket of yarn overflowed with gold needles sticking out from skeins of pink, yellow, and black fibers at the side of the soft, cushioned couch. Kitsaun and I shared a bedroom with two twin beds with stuffed animals on our pillows. Our family's station in life was humble, yet we had an upright piano, piano teacher, dance lessons, and friends and family to play card games, Monopoly, and hide-and-seek outside.

I never felt any lack or need except for the time I saw a shiny red Schwinn bicycle in the *Sears, Roebuck* catalog. In more than 1,500 pages, all I wanted was that bicycle. I dreamed of riding it in our neighborhood. Dad knew I wanted a bike and brought home a used matte red one from a secondhand shop. He smiled as he pushed the bike toward me. The look on my face must have been crestfallen. *"Do you like it, Dobs?"* he asked, using my pet name.

I swallowed hard and pulled a smile to my lips. *"Oh yes, Dad. Thank you,"* while noticing the rear bumper was rusty and bent. But off I rode pedaling my new/old two-wheeler, a girl with places to go.

Mom and Dad turned on the six o'clock news every night. We watched the Beatles arrive in San Francisco to perform at the Cow Palace with hundreds of young girls sobbing as the British musicians walked from their plane. There were news stories about the free-speech movement at University of California, Berkeley, and San Francisco State and anti-war protestors being dragged from campus buildings by city police. I sensed my parents' stress when they talked about protests around the country. At the time of the 1965 Selma to Montgomery March, which left activists beaten and bloodied, I was fourteen and began to think about joining the movement. Our family was outraged at the barbaric treatment of our sisters and brothers seeking equality by boycotting segregated businesses, rejecting unlawful voting suppression tactics, and racially motivated incarceration.

My stake in the movement was personal. My Black ancestors hailed from Louisiana: Thomas J. King and Sealand Davis, parents of my grandfather, Judge; Sanders Mitchell and Sealy Hoozer, parents of my grandmother, Sarah. My great-grandparents were born in the mid-1800s when census records for Black citizens were not kept, and the only family histories we had were recorded in our Bibles. Lynchings were commonplace in Louisiana and caused terror in the lives of Black families. Even a glance at a white person was cause for reprimand, legal action, or being hanged from a tree. Our interracial family's rights were in jeopardy, too, as we were ostracized and denounced by those who refused to accept desegregation.

There were rallies in front of the Federal Building in San Francisco and free-speech activists protested at Sproul Hall at UC Berkeley. It was a power-filled time of resisting status quo politics. Watching police violently attack demonstrators caused my body to shake with anger and fear. I was a sensitive child—an empath—and even hateful speech scared me. A seminal moment was when I was in the third grade and walked past schoolmates as one of them sneered, *"Your mama's as white as day, and your Daddy's as black as night."* I absorbed their contemptuous words like a knife slicing through my skin. When I told Mom and Dad, Dad's jaw tightened, and he said, *"If anyone says anything else, you pick up a brick and hit them over the head."*

Mom pulled me onto her lap and cooed in my ear, *"Those children know nothing about who you are, Deborah. Their words are from their ignorance.*" I wanted to believe her, but the children's comments stirred a fear in me that was rooted in the trauma I felt from stories told around the kitchen table. Their sneers activated my emotional alert system that told me I was in danger because of my brown skin, just as my grandparents had been in their church and my father in nightclubs in Texas and Oklahoma.

Dad and Mom were yin and yang in their reactions to society's inequities. It was quite different to be born Black in America than white. Mom had not been programmed as part of the caste system, but her balanced, egalitarian thinking couldn't ameliorate her husband's or daughters' experiences in an inequitable social order. She had compassion for people, especially those less fortunate than us, and diligently voted in every election, believing her ballot would make a difference. Dad voted, too, but was wary of governing systems because of unceasing discrimination and scrutiny on his life as a Black man.

Once he was pulled over by police when driving to his nightclub gig in Sunnyvale, Dad was on guard. "*What's the problem, officer?*" he asked, while rolling down his window.

"*Let me see your license,*" barked the white man.

When he saw Dad's name, the officer relaxed his shoulders. "*Oh, I've seen your name before on the marquee for Jack's Tavern. You're on your way to work?*" Dad was pardoned without a ticket for whatever offense the officer might have fabricated.

Dad used his mind to shield him from racism, statuesque against a system of tyranny toward Blacks. Mom spoke up and out with anyone who did not view us as equal. The love in our home was a shield from glares and bigoted words cast our way. From my parents' example, I learned to make my own homes sanctuaries from the troubled world.

———

MOM'S SKIN WAS RADIANT, like fresh fallen snow in sunlight. Sitting in church, I often stole a glance at her profile during the sermon, her button nose a dainty point between her high cheekbones. Her skin flushed as she sang hymns and clapped her thin hands, her eyes closed to allow Spirit's flow. She talked to everyone she met—on street corners or park benches—to ask how they were doing, and handed a dollar bill to women with children, even though we needed every dollar for ourselves. On Saturdays, one of her two days off from her job at Social Security, she made mac-and-cheese casseroles to take to the mothers of the church.

Nanny, nearly 100 years old with a voice like bamboo stalks rubbing together in the wind, was one of Mom's favorites. Kitsaun and I rode with Mom to deliver the meals, her lead foot taking us swiftly across the Bay Bridge into the neighborhood of two-story gingerbread houses in West Oakland. Nanny greeted us at the top of the stairs, wearing a pink housecoat. "*Well, well, Jody, girls, come on in,*" she said, beaming. Sometimes she wore her false teeth, and sometimes she didn't, and her lips fell in on her gums. Nanny shuffled to sit in her sunken side chair, eager to talk about the lives of church members and her faith.

Mom embraced the teachings of the Holiness Pentecostal church. She found solace in intercessory prayer—praying for others and being prayed for—believing healing would come as a result. Before church began, she sometimes crouched at the chancel rail, with her head tipped down to her folded hands. Uncle U.S. stood to her side, his hand on her shoulder, praying over her. Mom's skin was only a vessel for her bones, muscles, and heart. She was fortitude and righteousness, defiant of the status quo, with a generous sprinkling of caring and love for everyone in her life.

I don't know from whom she received her courageous heart, but of the five Willis sisters, Mom lived most fully with a sense of sufficiency and bravery, or so it seemed to me. I never saw her break down except at funerals. Maybe she cried about the oppression of racism with Uncle U.S.'s wife, Bitsy, who was her best friend and confidante. Mom fit seamlessly into the King family, embraced as a full member.

Her mother, Virgie—Mamaw to the grandchildren—was taciturn. If we saw her smile, it was a tight-lipped dash on her thin lips. When my children were born, I began compiling our scant genealogy records and found that Mamaw married "Shortie," Bennie Bertram Willis, in a horse and buggy at the age of fifteen. His family was moving away, and Mamaw said she would die if she couldn't move with him. Shortie was seventeen and very clever; he was also an individualist and a wanderer. He wrote poetry, could fix any car, and was fond of smoking and drinking.

The Willis family was from Georgia; Mamaw's parents, the Hudspeths, were from Arkansas. Mamaw's mother, Anna Lee Teaff, had died in childbirth when Mamaw was only ten years old. Her father, Joseph Franklin Hudspeth, was left with six children to raise. With one older brother, Mamaw must have assumed the role of mother to her younger siblings, including the twins who were born when her mother died. This information helped me understand her clenched jaw and stern face in photos, and why she thought she would die if she didn't marry Shortie and leave her life at home.

Shortie and Mamaw's first child, Mom's oldest sister, Nomi, was born when Mamaw was seventeen. Nita was born two years later, Dini two years after that, Aggie three years more, and Mom, the last of the five girls, two years after that when Mamaw was twenty-eight. The Willis clan lived in Texas, Arizona, and California, usually in a one-bedroom house. The five girls slept in one bed and worked in fields picking cotton in Texas or apricots and peaches in California. Mamaw sewed all their clothes.

They worked together, traveling around California in an old Model T. They dined on stewed tomatoes on saltine crackers for dinner. When they finally settled in Casa Grande, Arizona, Nomi and Nita worked at the five-and-dime so they could have money to buy bobby pins and lipstick. The girls took advantage of the Arizona sun by rubbing baby oil on their skin and lying out to get tans. When Mom told me this story, she shuddered thinking about the damage bronzing their paperwhite skin could have caused.

The oldest girls, Nomi and Nita, were more confident and adventurous than their parents appreciated. *"Dad worked at a used car lot,"* Mom said, *"and Nomi and Nita sneaked out one night, hot-wired a car, and drove to a dance. Dad found out, went to the dance, tapped Nita on the shoulder as if he were a young man asking her to dance, and dragged them both home by their hair."*

The five girls were strikingly attractive, like the glamorous movie stars of the 1940s, with blond or brunette waves to their shoulders and beguiling smiles. They painted their long legs with makeup when they could not afford hosiery, and when they went out, they adorned their small-waisted figures in cotton or velvet fitted dresses.

As youngsters, Mom and her four sisters spent Saturday mornings searching sidewalks and streets for gum, candy, and cigarette wrappers. *"We formed the tinfoil into big balls that my sisters sold to a salvage company,"* Mom said, *"and used the nickels to go to the afternoon movie matinee."*

Mom enjoyed learning and in high school, as she waited for an assignment to be returned, the teacher stood before them, homework papers in her hands. *"A's are as scarce as hen's teeth,"* she pronounced.

Mom turned this phrase over in her mind, imagining the mouth of a chicken, the pointy sharp beak pecking in the dirt, and realized hens didn't have teeth. She was snapped out of it when the teacher slapped her paper down on her desk with "A" marked boldly across the top.

The Willis daughters grew up knowing their grandmothers, but their male ancestry beyond Grandpa Joseph F. Hudspeth, Virgie's father, was not well-known. On hot summer days, they drove to Grandpa Hudspeth's farm in a touring car that had no windows. The sides were open and could be closed only by snapping pieces of canvas to isinglass. Grandpa Hudspeth was married to a woman they called Grandma Dean. She was his second wife and not their mother's mother, and the girls did not feel close to her. They spent afternoons in the orchard eating sweet peaches they picked from the trees. In the evenings, Grandpa Hudspeth played his violin, swaying his body as he pulled the bow across the strings.

I assumed my mother learned to pray in the Baptist church in which she was raised. But when I learned that Mom grew up in a small Arizona desert town and attended school with Native American and Mexican children, I wondered if she learned to pray under the great stretch of sky when she wandered outside, feeling the power of the universe above her head and beneath her feet.

When Nita graduated high school, she moved to Chicago. By day, she worked for the federal government and at night she checked coats in a nightclub. Mom graduated high school and followed her older sister to the Midwest metropolis, working the same jobs. They both sent the balance of their wages home to help their mother. Nita was dating a saxophone player who introduced Mom to Dad. I can picture the stage lights on Dad, illuminating him and his guitar as he played, and Mom watching him with a flutter in her heart.

My mother was independent and innovative. Her partnership with Dad was as equals—advanced for the 1950s when many wives stayed at home raising children and followed their husband's rule. Mom worked at Social Security, bringing home a steady paycheck. If Dad displeased Mom, he knew about it. They went head-to-head in arguments because she felt equal to him and knew her opinion was valued. She was bold in her conversation and a feminist in beliefs and comportment. On weekends, she often wanted to get out of the city. *"Saunders,"* she said, *"let's drive to Sonoma."* Dad got his keys, and we piled into the car for an afternoon escapade. Her love for Dad was ardent and fearless; her search for knowledge, both spiritual and intellectual, was keen. She took anthropology classes at night at City College when Kitsaun and I were in high school, all while working full time, and kept a stack of mysteries and books about health on her nightstand, reading every night and on weekends.

Mom was vastly different from her sisters. She didn't drink, and lived her faith, praying throughout her life; as far as I saw, none of my aunts attended church. Mom trusted science and studies about diet. None of my friends' mothers made carrot juice and cooked brown rice instead of white rice like Mom did.

I once asked her, *"What opened your mind to alternative healing modalities, yoga, and the organic foods you introduced to our family when we were teens?"*

"My dad rolled and smoked unfiltered cigarettes, and he died at fifty-two," she told me. *"Both of my grandfathers died before I was born. We were poor and didn't have access to fresh, healthy food, and getting to eat fruits and vegetables was rare. When I was a young girl, my big treat was a banana on Saturdays."*

Having so little to eat gave Mom a fervor for good nutrition and informed her progressive ideas about diet and health—Mom was smart and inquisitive. Her self-assurance originated from the matriarchal family in which she was born—five daughters, a hardworking and indefatigable mother, and a father who wrote poetry to his wife and girls.

I have a faded page of torn lined paper with my grandfather's writing from 1936:

> *I realized I had passed another milestone,*
> *And was living in the afternoon of my life.*
> *And it's not what you send that fills my heart with joy,*
> *But it's to know that you have remembered the old gray-haired boy.*
> *A little keepsake I had, I prized more than any, was a little card.*
> *I think a Father's Day card; one of the first my angels ever sent me.*
> *I think it was way back in Alpine, Texas days.*
> *It must have cost one cent, maybe better than that,*
> *It may have been a two-for-five cents class.*
> *Anyway, it's worth a million dollars to me.*

I sense the love my grandfather had for his daughters in this poem and in a black-and-white photograph where he sat on the front of a horse with four of his five girls behind him, Mamaw at the other end; Mom must not have been born. Their faces were somber beneath bowl haircuts, and Mamaw was the only one not looking into the camera. She had the same haircut and the same solemn expression. How could I have expected my grandmother to smile? She had a difficult life working in fields raising five girls and being widowed at fifty after being married to my grandfather for 35 years, a man who called her "the flower deep in his heart" in a handwritten Mother's Day poem. She was a survivor and passed this skill to her daughters, who all started working right after high school to send money to support her.

I think my mother's surety to live as she believed came from Mamaw. Mom stoically weathered the intense oppression she experienced marrying Dad. She never talked about the racism she encountered walking down streets with him unless we asked. She raised her chin and said, "*It wasn't that bad,*" as if being spit on by a white man in Chicago who saw her leaving Dad's side wasn't an atrocious act.

She was never androcentric and was always vexed by the patriarchal constraints of society. Mom preferred women doctors, dentists, and authors to their male counterparts. More than once, she took time off from work to catch a bus across San Francisco to meet with high school counselors when Kitsaun or I were sent to detention for speaking out of turn or talking back in class. She always took our side.

She was prepared to march to neighbors' homes to defend us if any child or parent touched my sister or me or called us racist words. Mom never felt she needed to explain the Black man whose arm she clutched and was ever vigilant to defend and protect the two brown girls she had birthed. She dismissed people's ignorance with a hard stare. Because of her strong mothering, I never needed another woman to show me the way.

MY FATHER WAS ALWAYS A KING TO ME, not only in last name, but in stature, assuredness, and grandness. I looked up to Dad with respect; he didn't coddle Kitsaun and me but told us, "*Look around yourselves. Don't talk to strangers. Don't open the front door for anyone.*"

He was a head taller than other parents who picked up their children from school, his face stern until he spotted us walking toward him and light shone from his eyes. Even when he didn't speak, I felt Dad's love.

We often visited his sister, Daisy, and brothers Ulysses Sr., Judge, and Jay, although the latter two only when we traveled to Grandmother's Chowchilla farm. Uncle U.S. took over the pastorship of Christ Holy Sanctified Church at 1735 Seventh Street in Oakland when their father died. Daisy lived in Berkeley but had lived in Los Angeles and worked for Paramount Studios in her twenties. She was given acting roles of a dancing girl or maid because of her dark skin. She carried herself like a princess, perhaps because she was the darling of the family as the only girl child. The Kings were creatives: Uncle Jay was an inventor who mixed a recipe for shoe polish that was stolen from him; Uncle Judge was a farmer who tended peach trees, cows, and chickens; and Dad became a well-known blues and jazz guitarist and singer, whose two-part "SK Blues" recording earned him international acclaim.

When I was a child, my image of Saunders King was that he was taller than the Monterey Pine outside our bedroom window. His voice was a velvet ribbon of tenor tones, and his blond Gibson guitar was an extension of his craft when he sang his favorite songs, "Big Fat Butterfly" and "What's Your Story Morning Glory?"

Pressed wool slacks, and unwrinkled cotton dress shirts worn with a tie and jacket on Sundays for church, were his uniform. Dad wore t-shirts only on the tennis court, and those were polo style, the de rigueur tennis attire.

Each morning, I watched Dad stand in front of the bathroom mirror to shave. When the weekly show from the flamboyant musician Liberace was on, he had the TV on in the living room so he could listen. The morning Dad was on our TV on Ralph Gleason's show *Jazz Casual* singing "Summertime," I was rapt on the living room floor watching. Because Dad sang and played his guitar every day in our home, I knew he was a musician but seeing him on TV gave me a thrill.

"Are other people watching Dad?" I wondered. He kept his music life separate from his family to protect us from the ways of the men he knew so well. Dad distanced himself from the church his father and mother built when he started his career because the Holiness church did not approve of secular music. He wanted to respect their teachings while he pursued his love of performing.

Dad's musical ear developed growing up in the Pentecostal church, listening to soloists in the choir and his mother and father singing. He studied violin and voice, learning to read music at Prescott Elementary School in Oakland under the tutelage of his music teacher, Mrs. Forsythe. Dad recalled, *"Every time I brought the violin from school, I would be in a fight before I got home."* He abandoned the violin for the guitar when he graduated; his first purchase was an acoustic Epiphone.

He was hired to deliver suits for Holsten Holmes Tailors in San Francisco across the street from NBC Radio at 111 Sutter. He told the tailors, *"I'm going to work at NBC. I'm going to get a job there singing."* The son of the owner asked, *"Can you sing?"*

"So, I sang for them," Dad recalled, *"and they saw I had a certain amount of talent."*

At twenty-five, Dad auditioned for and was hired by NBC Radio singing tenor with the gospel quartet, Southern Harmony Four. Monday through Saturday mornings, they sang on the program, *Cross Cuts from the O' Log of the Day.* His fellow musicians were three suave Black men: Eugene Anderson, Alvin Nurse, and William Barber. The show featured the sounds of a live crosscut saw slicing through a real log in the studio, along with "live" tweeting birds and Dr. Cross, a white "colonel" character discussed current events with the quartet, who acted as a work crew of loggers. Dad also became a staff artist for NBC, where he would stand by in the hallway ready to take the mic and perform if telegraph lines from shows broadcasting from New York lost the signal. At that time, more than 28 million American households owned a radio. No wonder Dad longed to be on NBC.

In 1938, Dad became leader of a house band at the iconic Sweets Ballroom on Fourteenth and Franklin in Oakland called The Aristocrats of Swing. As he later said in *Sights and Sounds: Essays in Celebration of West Oakland,* *"Les Hite gave me my first break; the first solo I sang with the band was 'Stardust.' They didn't think I could sing that kind of music, and I did very well with it."*

Most of the musicians Dad played with held full-time jobs in a variety of positions, such as insurance salesperson, electrician, redcap porter, and radio announcer. Some had attended university; all voraciously loved playing music and often finished their evening gigs and moved to another location to "jam" into the early morning hours. *"I made a lot of friends in downtown San Francisco. All of them came to see me when they found out I was working in clubs,"* Dad said.

Dad's first wife, Augustine, with whom he had two sons, Saunders Jr. and Gilbert, was an elegant Black woman from Oakland. We grew up seeing the boys occasionally, and it was fun to have older brothers who arm wrestled us while they teased us about our skinny legs. I was captivated by Augustine's russet brown skin and coiffed hair that reminded me of Aunt Daisy's glamour.

Dad's second wife was a mystery to us. I supposed it was normal not to discuss past spouses, but the words "suicide" and "jumped from a window" were phrases we heard whispered. As it turned out, Margery Marston, a redhead and graduate of Mills College, and daughter of the owner of the US Grant Hotel in San Francisco, married Dad in 1939 in Seattle, where interracial marriage was legal. In 1942, she was found dead in their bathtub, her wrists slit and a glass of poison on the counter. The unofficial story was that she was devastated by rumors and her own suspicions of Dad's infidelities and took her life.

Dad never mentioned a word about her, yet I wondered how heartbroken he must have been and how he must have carried the loss in the core of his being. I identified with Margery's pain, not because I experienced infidelity in my marriage but because I felt the depth of her love for my father and imagined that she did not feel cherished. Relationships often bring suffering and sorrow after initial thrills and happiness. Thinking my father did not adore Margery more than the aphrodisiac of lust hurt my heart.

He met Mom five years later. Mom became Dad's third wife, sixteen years his junior, married when she was twenty-two and he was thirty-eight. Dad's life experience as a professional musician and twice-married father must have engulfed her innocence and unworldliness.

Anti-miscegenation laws were still in effect in seventeen states, including California, and Dad returned to Seattle with Mom to marry. Legally, their interracial union was not recognized in California, even though Dad made sure there was a lawful record in Washington state. Mom's maiden name "Willis" was recorded on my birth certificate, a moral blow to her and disrespectful of my parents' love.

Kitsaun was twenty-two months older than me, and I was the tag-along. When Dad drove Kitsaun to kindergarten, I was in the back seat of the Chevrolet, bouncing along for the early morning outing. Afterward he sometimes visited friends in the Fillmore District, leaving me locked in the car reading. Even as I wrote this, I saw my small body sitting in the car, looking up from my book and peering through the window, waiting to see Dad walk toward me. It was unfathomable to think the world was safe enough to leave a child alone in a car then—or today.

For his daughters' fun, Dad would drive speedily up and over the Dolores Street hills, taking us to Mel's Drive-In, our stomachs flying up into our throats while we laughed hysterically and screamed, *"Faster, Dad, faster!"* He and Mom were in the audience at our choir concerts, dance recitals, and high school football games when I was cheerleader. He kept an invisible moat around us so no boys could penetrate his protective wall. We never saw Dad perform live with other musicians except at church, but we grew up in the aura of his musicality. His guitar leaned on the side of the couch, and he picked it up, sheet music on the coffee table, and fingered tunes every day. By the age of five, I hummed along to sophisticated jazz tunes I'd heard since I was a baby. Dad's guitar playing blessed our family with tender moods and an atmosphere of imagination and soulful style.

Dad endured years of racist policies and hostilities in his musical career yet earned lavish praise for his talent on recordings and stage. He was labeled a blues musician but didn't restrict himself to that genre.

In newspaper ads from the late 1940s, San Francisco's legendary club, Savoy Tivoli, billed him as part of "The Greatest Sepia Show on the Coast," listing the "suave rhythms of Saunders King" just below headliner Art Tatum. He shared the stage with Billie Holiday when she came to town and was promoted as "The Red Hot Rhythms of Saunders King." *San Francisco Chronicle* writer Lee Hildebrand quoted singer Joe Williams, saying his distinctive vocal style was influenced by San Francisco-based singer-guitarist-bandleader Saunders King. *"He's a coal-black, beautiful sort of a guy . . . I could understand the lyrics . . . besides, he sang with great feeling."*

Dad told us, *"My reason for singing the blues was because people would request it. It wasn't hard to improvise blood, sweat, and tears... so consequently, I became a blues singer. All my life, that's what I wanted—to sing."*

Dad was the kind of handsome that turned people's heads when they passed. Women noticed his thick black moustache and bright, sparkling eyes, along with his musical talents. Mom never appeared to worry, keeping her life vibrant with us girls, her friends, and church. She loved to tell the story of Billie Holiday telling Daisy, *"You're cute but Saunders is beautiful."*

The Fillmore District was known as the "Harlem of the West" in the 1940s and 1950s. Dad loved the Fillmore. It wasn't just a street—it was home to men, women, and children who identified as Black, loved all that was Black, and fancied blues and jazz. There were barbershops and beauty salons, newsstands, nightclubs, churches, restaurants, hot dog stands, and record shops. It was an entire world.

Dad recorded his biggest hit, *SK Blues*, in 1942 with Rhythm Records, a San Francisco recording company owned by Dave Rosenbaum. He later recorded with Decca and Aladdin. We had these records on 78 RPM vinyl discs stacked in brown paper sleeves on the console. My favorite songs to listen to were "I've Had My Moments," "Why Was I Born?" "Get Yourself Another Fool," and "Imagination." Dad's sound and vocal technique were unique to him, and I swooned hearing his emotive tenor voice with buttery oscillation. He not only had a gift for enchanting people with his singing, but he also had a talent for molding the musicians in his bands into a cohesive unit that moved audiences to dancing the jitterbug and swing.

Dad drove to the Russian River, seventy miles north of San Francisco and a popular destination in summer when city dwellers spent weeks vacationing in rented cabins along Del Rio Woods beach. On Saturdays he performed at Palomar Bar and Dance with the house orchestra. Couples moved their feet on the polished maple dance floor while the musicians played swing tunes.

I wished I'd had the opportunity to see Dad in his element. I have photos of him gliding across the stage while he sang, and of him holding that bulbous Gibson guitar with his left hand clamped around the neck. He once said, *"What is blues? Woman and man. Man and woman. If you haven't lived it, you can't play it. I think blues is jazz and jazz is blues."*

In the 1950s and '60s, Dad played in a nightclub in Sunnyvale on weekends. He left our house for the club, wearing sunglasses and a sharkskin suit. Our family was unique for that time. Our friends' fathers went to work each morning while their mothers stayed home. Our mother went to work, and our father stayed home.

I learned through this example that life did not have to be traditional to be good. Our parents taught Kitsaun and me that we could be different. We could be biracial when only one other person in our class was. We could have a father who picked us up after school in a sea of mothers. We could think and live differently. There was something to be said for our name: We were Kings. This gave me confidence in who I was despite systems of discrimination. My parents wouldn't focus on it, so I learned not to focus on it, although it was always simmering beneath my calm façade.

Dad's luminous eyes sharply minded the world around his family; the way he cocked his head to listen to Mom, Kitsaun, our friends, and me showed us he was interested not only in what we had to say, but how we were choosing to live. His eloquent words and the way he chuckled at memories of musicians in his band remained a lighthouse for me. Much of his life was private, even to us, but his walk declared his bravery and fearlessness. I believed he could face any foe.

Dad was born in Louisiana, Mom was born in Texas; Dad loved the heat, Mom loved San Francisco fog. Jazz chords seeped from Dad's pores, gospel songs from Mom's lips. Dad walked with a sophisticated swagger; Mom walked forward through life swinging her arms with dogged determination.

If the King family had a coat of arms, the symbols would be warriors who lived with generosity and loyalty, which is the foundation of my life.

3

THE ALCHEMY OF LIFE

Kitsaun and I grew up exploring San Francisco's ubiquitous cultural settings—some grand like Coit Tower, the white column rising from Telegraph Hill with its colorful murals of agriculture, industry, immigration, and social class that looked like they were painted in chalk. Others were unpretentious like the Japanese Tea Garden in Golden Gate Park where we crouched at low tables and drank warm green tea in white ceramic teacups and cracked open quarter-moon fortune cookies to discover our fates.

"I'm a native of San Francisco," we both proudly declared whenever asked where we were born. As girls, we peered into aquariums at Fisherman's Wharf and watched lobsters clawing at the glass, trying to escape. Afterward, we ate at Alioto's, where Dad donned a white plastic bib to eat cracked crab. We laughed at the sight of this stylish man wearing such an amusing covering over his shirt.

We jumped rope and scraped our knees climbing the steep hill at the top of our street where we looked out over our bejeweled city. San Francisco gave me an identity as a citizen of a complex, diverse world where people of many ethnicities spoke languages from around the globe.

As teenagers, we and our friends attended rallies and marches for civil rights, knowing that America had to change old patterns of exclusion and caste systems. San Francisco's musical culture was vibrant and eclectic, with free outdoor concerts in Golden Gate Park that we attended. After high school, Kitsaun attended City College. Two years later, when it was time for me to go to college, my friends went off to UC Berkeley and San Francisco State, but I had met a charismatic musician five years my senior and enrolled in Cal State Dominguez Hills near Los Angeles to be with him. As nerve-racking as this was for my parents, I set off with my suitcases, with every intention of graduating. But the relationship was unhealthy, and the man became abusive. I returned to San Francisco, my parents wrapping me in their love. I enrolled at San Francsico State University to continue my studies, sometimes borrowing Mom and Dad's Dodge Challenger to drive to campus. My English courses included readings by Flannery O'Connor and Maya Angelou, and memories of the man I left dissipated into the distance like a vapor trail behind an airplane.

I was soon feeling my true self and blessed to be home. Friends invited me to a Tower of Power concert and backstage I met Carlos Santana, a skinny, long-haired guitar player. Although I was wary of becoming involved with another musician, I was only twenty-one, and young enough to believe Carlos was different from my former boyfriend. He asked me out, and we explored San Francisco in his black Volvo hatchback. He had a spiritual practice of meditation and was soft-spoken, not at all flamboyant. We enjoyed mutual interests: I practiced Hatha yoga, and he shared his morning meditations on Paramhansa Yogananda's yoga teachings with me. We fell in love, and I was swept into his life, traveling the world and living the music. Eventually, it was too hard for me to continue my studies, and I dropped out of college.

Carlos and I were dedicated to meditating early each morning and became acolytes of a guru who urged us to open a vegetarian restaurant we named Dipti Nivasto to promote his spiritual path and share the message of peace. The guru wanted us to marry saying it would enhance our spiritual growth, and we went to the Marin County Superior Court for the marriage license. A few weeks later, the guru performed a spiritual ceremony for us with our mothers and sisters in attendance. Carlos and I followed the guru for ten years until we wanted to start a family. This was discouraged on the guru's path, so we departed and began a new chapter in our lives.

We had three wonderful children—Salvador, Stella, and Angelica—and took them on tour with us and encouraged their creative proclivities. My days were filled with guiding them to seek spiritual values and supporting them in school. Mom and I volunteered in their classrooms and chaperoned on field trips. Each one was unique in spirit and creativity: As they grew, Salvador chose music as his passion and expression, Stella was a strong athlete who played volleyball, and Angelica was a gifted writer. Whenever possible, I sought learning for myself and took writing and business management courses, continuing to expand my knowledge in the areas most important to me.

When Angelica was five, Stella ten, and Salvador twelve, Carlos fired his managers and we took over the duties of managing the band. Carlos was CEO/owner. I was the COO/owner and vice president, working with attorneys and accountants. We hired Kitsaun to work with the fan club and eventually she interfaced with our public relations firm and interacted with the record company. Carlos and I started the Milagro Foundation, and I was vice president of this non-profit that funded organizations supporting children in the arts, education, and health. I was as devoted to our family and business as I had been to the guru and my vegetarian restaurant, eking out time for my own passions after my workday ended.

Carlos's music was the center of our lives. Over the years, he had extramarital dalliances that were heartbreaking to me, eroding my confidence and making me feel unloved. After confrontations and arguments, he asked forgiveness and pledged not to stray, but my heart was always on alert. My parents loved Carlos, and I never shared my pain with them. Perhaps keeping the family together is what kept *me* together. His career was always manageable—until he won nine Grammys in 2000 for the *Supernatural* album. After that, requests for interviews, television appearances, and more concerts increased. Carlos was away from home more than ever, and I understood the term "superstar."

I focused on improving my writing, attended workshops, and joined a writing group. My goal was to finish a memoir that told my coming-of-age story. Daily, I also interfaced with attorneys and accountants, overseeing budgets and signing checks to pay office and touring bills. I led weekly staff meetings, wrote the Santana Fan Newsletter, listened to project updates, and discussed requests from the music industry for Carlos's time. I didn't need to take time away from my work as chief operations officer to write a book. I could do both.

Yet once, after he returned from a grueling concert tour, Carlos stood at my upstairs office door and watched me at my desk, typing my manuscript. I could feel his tension.

"Are those sloppy joes all we have for dinner?"

I finished typing the sentence and looked up. *"The kids love them,"* I answered.

"Well, I don't."

My thoughts were many: He was certainly able to pick up dinner from his favorite restaurants for himself and the children, if he wanted. But the concert touring lifestyle catered to him on the road and created a system of helplessness when he was home. He was accustomed to having his crew provide for his every need. I didn't want that to be a part of our home life. Most importantly, we were nearing the 21st century, and women, certainly those who worked outside the home, were no longer obligated to be the sole caretakers of children.

I swiveled in my chair to face him, anger flashing from his eyes.

"I need to finish this chapter before my writing class. Can you please manage your dinner?"

Even as I spoke the words, I felt guilty for not jumping up and running out to get the dinner he wanted. I hated that we had this unequal dynamic in which I was still fighting to gain his respect as someone worthy of creating. I treated myself as if my writing came a distant third, after family and the band's business. I wanted to change the dynamic.

There is a wizardry in the lives of the famous—the world is marketed a version of how the artist wants to be seen, often with charm and awe.

People watch those who are famous to escape from reality and daydream of what a glamorous, larger-than-life existence would be like.

But the excitement of fame is only part of the story. There is an ordinariness to everyone's life.

Carlos speaks of angels all around us, universal peace, divine love. He believes in these concepts, meditates, and reads spiritual books. Spellbinding energy floats in the air during concerts when he fingers his guitar and sends songs into the galaxy.

But he is human with the struggles we all have, including the challenge to live the beliefs he espouses. I learned to tiptoe through the house when he first returned from a tour, making sure he had the rest he needed, even when the children were very young, and I was exhausted, too. I am a morning person, and he comes alive at night, when he would leave the children and me to go to his studio. He knew how to claim what he needed and didn't think it necessary to alter his life for us. And I had always considered his music life the most important focus of our family's dynamic, even though this devotion required me to minimize my interests and worth.

I turned back to my computer and held my breath until he left the doorway. I was as dedicated to his career as he was and loved my work in management, but I also loved being in silence with my imagination, and the steady scratch of my pen in my journal or the clicking of computer keys beneath my fingers when I wrote. Something was happening in my writing, something that made me feel alive, and I wanted his encouragement.

A few days later, he was rested from his tour and came into the kitchen, putting his arms around me. *"You give me so much. I feel like I've been in the desert."*

"Hmmm," I said. As if now that his tour was finished and demands on him had eased, he could be soft again, ready to hug and interact, and we could be a couple. It was always on his terms, in his time.

I longed for him to see my world. I continued searching for my own road to travel with my writing, a place that came from the strength of women in my family who worked in government jobs and were not stay-at-home mothers, from the voices of women who did not succumb to sacrificing their creativity for their partners'.

Each day the hunger to write, to put my thoughts and the mosaic of my life to paper vibrated stronger in me. Through rewrite after rewrite, I knew that I wanted to stand in the patina of my words.

———————

Space Between the Stars was published after seven years of hard work to define my narrative and share the truths of my life. When I read an abridged version for my audiobook, I imagined my words floating out into the world, carrying me to a new life. Becoming a published author was more powerful than I had dreamed.

March 3, 2005, was my first book signing. I drove to Book Passage, where writing my memoir had begun, arriving early to meet with co-owner Elaine Petrocelli. Her sleek chin-length hair framed her smile as she greeted me with a hug: *"I am so happy to have you here."*

She led me to a table, where I began signing books to place on shelves after that night's reading. People filed into the large room, sitting in folding chairs lined up in two sections. I greeted friends and acquaintances, the space filling to standing room only. A hazy, surreal light enveloped me as I climbed the two stairs to the podium and began to read my words. I had fought hard to finish this memoir, while developing my self-image, letting go of expectations to be the perfect mother and wife, believing that my journey had a purpose. I had climbed a mountain to reach this spectacular place of standing in my own life.

Seeing faces looking back at mine, I wanted nothing more than to live in the illumining strength my mother and father had given me, and that was not to have value only as a wife. I introduced my mother in the front row of the audience, and everyone stood to applaud her. Mom didn't stand but waved her arm as if to say, *"Don't pay attention to me. This is my daughter's night."*

This is how my mom mothered—like the volunteers on Hawaii's beaches who watch green sea turtles swim horizontal in the waves, feeding on algae for hours. When the hard-shelled creatures tire and swim to shore to rest, the volunteers encircle them in red protective rope so no one will disturb them or bring them harm. Mom had watched me swimming in my life, and now that I was standing up in my story, she was close by.

I felt privileged and complete, full as I had never been, with *Space Between the Stars* out in the world. Before, my creative spirit had felt like tea leaves dried in the hot sun. Now, the clean flowing water of acceptance and understanding had softened me, and the true power of living my words in the world opened my heart.

I traveled to fifty-five readings and book signings in bookstores, book fairs, libraries, churches, and private gatherings. Every event, every interview, every word I spoke brought me closer to redefining my life. I had an insight that the world was my monastery, the temple where I could pray, write, study, read, learn, and love. Years ago, I had thought I wanted to go to India to serve in Mother Teresa's Missionaries of Charity. I had held her work as the pinnacle of human dedication. Once Carlos and I started our family, I knew my work was in the world as a householder, as Indian culture describes homemakers. Connecting with readers of my memoir gave me a sense of how art could be service, and each question and comment was a hug of encouragement on my journey.

The book brought a sense of good fortune to my heart.

MoAD DREAMS

Now that most of my events for *Space Between the Stars* were local, I was eager for new work, and that's when celebrated journalist and television newscaster Belva Davis called me. I had known Belva for many years and held deep respect for her as an interviewer and newscaster and revered her as the first African-American woman to become a television reporter on the West Coast.

"Hello, Deborah, I'm so glad to have made contact with you," Belva said. *"We're building a new museum in San Francisco: the Museum of the African Diaspora."*

I was immediately curious. When I was a child, Africa was described as a far off undeveloped continent, not the birthplace of civilization. Images of Africans were stereotypically barbaric, and we were not taught that royal clans or thriving people lived in large cities as well as on fertile lands. Art and artifacts were stolen during colonialism, looted from Native and African lands.

Belva told me that trustees of this new museum were committed to telling an accurate story of the diaspora and bringing art from the continent. *"We'll have exhibitions showcasing the history, art, and cultural richness that resulted from the dispersal of Africans throughout the world,"* she said.

It felt important, a correction of the history that was taught not only to me but to everyone—adding dimension to the human understanding of a highly misunderstood culture.

"This museum is a grand idea, and I hope you'll join me on the board of directors," Belva said. I would have participated in anything Belva asked me to. She was one of the most courageous women I knew who was not in my family. When she began her journalism career in 1964, she covered the Republican National Convention in San Francisco, the only Black journalist in the arena. Taunting spectators yelled, *"Get out of here, nig—r bitch*!" throwing bottles and cans at her and her colleague. From that frightening, humiliating experience, Belva went on to interview five presidents; Huey Newton, leader of the Black Panthers; Robert Kennedy; Cesar Chavez; Spike Lee; and Fidel Castro. She has won eight Emmy awards.

"I'm honored," I told her. *"Can you tell me where it is located?"*

"I welcome giving you a tour," she said. *"We're still under construction south of Market Street in San Francisco, part of the St. Regis Hotel. Please let me know when you can fit a tour into your schedule."*

Belva was president of the board of directors, and I was intrigued and eager to see if I could join this project that would bring a more diverse art culture to the city.

I received documents to read before my visit. The redevelopment agency documents stated: "The Museum of the African Diaspora, a California nonprofit public benefit corporation (MoAD), is planning a unique cultural and museum facility to create an experience of the journeys, accomplishments, and achievements of the peoples from the African continent who have been transported throughout the world."

The museum facility would consist of about 20,000 square feet located on the last vacant parcel in Yerba Buena Gardens. The St. Regis Museum Tower structure would combine residential, commercial, and retail spaces. I drove to the city and met Belva and members of the team.

The contractor placed a hard hat in my hands, and I followed the group inside the unfinished building. Cement walls and a staircase led to floors that would soon display art.

I agreed to join the board and became involved before the museum was completed. The legacy of African Americans at the forefront of the project represented a tribute to my father's heritage and our family's years of living in San Francisco's Ingleside and Lakeview neighborhoods. Being included in the formation of the museum felt like an official seal of belonging.

Belva said, *"The museum aims to change the way people view the modern world and global family by looking at the 'connectivity' of cultures. The museum is not a collecting museum but will host travel exhibitions as well as shows it organizes. It will sponsor educational programs for students and website outreach to collect stories of the diaspora."*

When the doors opened in December 2005, the façade of the building sported floor-to-ceiling windows and a bright orange canopy. Through the large front windows, on the opposite wall, you could see a nearly three-story face of an African child—an eight-year-old from Ghana, taken by the great photographer Chester Higgins. The image was an artistic rendition—a mosaic of more than 2,000 photographs of people from around the world, which was a representation of the African diaspora.

The first exhibition, "Linkages and Themes in the African Diaspora: Selections from the Eileen Harris Norton and Peter Norton Contemporary Art Collections," included thirty-nine works—in photography, painting, mixed-media, video, and new genre—by artists Hew Locke, Willie Cole, Glenn Ligon, Malick Sidibe, Kara Walker, Chris Ofili, Fred Wilson, Isaac Julien, and Albert Chong. A mixed-media piece, "Bye, Bye Blackbird" by Los Angeles artist Alison Saar, was a metal suitcase, lit by neon, underneath a harness of wings made of leather shoe soles. Two untitled twelve-color silk-screen works by Iona Rozeal Brown—portraits of a Japanese male and female in dreadlocks and masking, representing the appropriation of hip-hop culture by Japanese youth—were hung strategically on the walls in radical splendor.

Ancient stone tools from Tanzania exhibited in glass cases were on loan from the British Museum. *"We have the oldest objects from the British Museum in London,"* then Executive Director Denise Bradley said. *"They're loaning us stone tools from Africa, which are nearly 2 million years old, and we'll allow people to handle the objects, which will be an important part of the exhibit."*

As a member of the board, I rolled up my sleeves and participated in choices and decisions about budgets, programs, and the direction of the museum.

Members of the board of directors were executives at corporations like Wells Fargo Bank, Dignity Health, and Kaiser Permanente and championed MoAD to receive significant donations. Over the next few years, the community became more invested in the diasporic richness of exhibitions and the museum's acclaimed MoAD in the Classroom (MIC) educational outreach program.

Every fall, the museum hosted a gala, each with a different theme and honorees. In 2014, I was vice chair of the board of directors and co-hosted the gala with Wilkes Bashford, the elegant clothier with a high-end eponymous store on Sutter Street. Wilkes knew everyone in San Francisco's high tier of politics, sports, journalism, and glitterati. He was a city booster and the board president of the War Memorial and Performing Arts Center, home of the San Francisco Ballet, the San Francisco Opera, and the San Francisco Symphony.

Our Lifetime Achievement honoree was Richard Mayhew, African-American-Native-American landscape painter, illustrator, and arts educator. His near-abstract paintings had adorned museums and galleries since 1957 and could be viewed at the de Young Museum in San Francisco.

We met to plan the gala over lunch at Le Central, the French Bistro on Bush Street. I arrived, and Wilkes, wearing round black glasses with blue-tinted lenses, greeted me with a warm smile and a hug. As we sat at his table and had a delicious meal, I looked around at the brick walls and brass bar and felt like I was in Paris. Wilkes drank his signature Campari while we discussed strategies for reaching new VIPs and the wording for a letter we would send out asking supporters to donate $15,000 per table.

Each time I saw Wilkes, I loved him more—his appreciation for life poured from his being. On the evening of the gala, he and I stood arm-in-arm, greeting many of the 375 attendees, me wearing a floor-length black gown I purchased at his atelier. Flashes from cameras recorded board members, Executive Director Linda Harrison, and guests in their finery—MoAD moments became moments to treasure.

Under the leadership of current Executive Director Monetta White, MoAD continues to expand its global reach. Programs include an African Book Club, Artist Talks, Emerging Artists Program, Chef-in-Residence, Poet-in-Residence, and an African Literary Award. The museum has doubled its budget; and increased its digital audience. Although I no longer serve on the board of directors, I remain as thrilled as I was when asked to join in 2005, proud of MoAD's jewel of a museum in the city of my birth. Belva was always involved, adding her poise and talent for raising funds to our efforts.

The museum underwent a renovation, adding a new room so that exhibitions could expand. The mission was updated as well: "*To place the contemporary art and artists of the African Diaspora at the center of the global cultural conversation.*"

I continue to visit and walk through the ever-evolving space, touring the landscape of spirit and earth, standing before paintings and sculptures that provide visual depictions of imaginations rich with a consciousness of Blackness. It is immensely gratifying to have believed in this museum from the beginning. I wish I had kept the hard hat I wore on my first visit. It would mean so much.

5

A MORE RADIANT FORM

It came as a surprise when my parents began to age. Dad and Mom had always been healthy and robust—eager to travel with us around the world. Dad performed on stage with Santana twice, once when Salvador was just a baby and Carlos introduced him at the Budokan in Tokyo to sing "Stardust," the same song he had performed with the Aristocrats of Swing in Oakland. Chester Thompson and Tom Coster made the keyboards swing, and the audience clapped and screamed. Dad was still a "cool cat" as jazz musicians say, and although his voice was not as strong as it had been in his early years, it was full with vibrato and emotional resonance. Seeing the performance made up for all the years I had missed seeing Dad play. I adored my parents and spent hours engaged in conversations and enjoyed the children with them. Our family was blessed to have both sets of the children's grandparents close by—Carlos's in Danville, my parents four miles away.

In the mid-1980s, Carlos and I purchased a two-and-a-third-acre lot on Bay Way, a street on a cul-de-sac in San Rafael. Soon after, Mom and Dad built a two-bedroom home on the hill above our house, and Carlos built a studio on the property, where his guitars, drums, gold records, and memorabilia were housed. Our gardeners planted a vegetable garden, hundreds of plants, including roses, azaleas, ferns, butterfly bushes, and poppies. They hand-built a koi pond in the center of it all with a bench where we could sit feeling the peace of the garden. There was no fence between the three structures, and we could walk to Mom and Dad's, behind the pond to the studio, and down flagstone steps to our house. We had a small shed for tools and soil-enhancement supplies, where the children sometimes burrowed when playing hide-and-seek.

Mom and Dad's house had its own gate and driveway on the street that curved behind us. On her weekly errands, Mom would back her blue Camry swiftly out of their garage onto the pebbled drive. As a fair-skinned goddess of compassion and love, she would glance over her left shoulder to make sure the sunflower stalks and squash remained a safe distance from her bumper. Shifting the gear into drive, she would shoot down the hill, past the sloshing waves of San Francisco Bay to the library for a new mystery or to Avanti Salon for a brown tint on her chin-length hair.

When Salvador was eleven, Mom taught him how to back the Camry out of the garage, and she was delighted in the knowledge that they were getting away with something daring I knew nothing about. Mom believed the kids should be able to drive and do chores like sweeping out her garage, folding laundry and putting away her groceries.

She loved to stand on her deck, pruning ruffled peach-colored roses as the bay breeze cooled her. She taught Stella to pinch off the dry petals of the African violets in her kitchen window. Likewise, she never pruned the reality she saw and spoke quick words of truth all her life.

When Dad suffered a stroke, we were all shaken. Kitsaun and I helped drive him to physical therapy and doctor's appointments, and Mom called me often to run up the hill to help. The saddest part was that Dad wouldn't pick up his guitar. Mom would lift it and ask, *"Saunders, won't you please try?"* He shook his head. *"No, Jo."* He suffered from aphasia, and his digital dexterity was slow. I could only imagine how his brain might jumble our conversation, or how the songs he once played without thinking were now sitting in some strange waiting room of his mind.

Grief sat in Mom's lungs, exacerbating her shortness of breath. She always had a weakness in her lungs, maybe asthma, but had never received a diagnosis and never used an inhaler.

Mom was the last living member of the Willis clan; all four of her sisters had died. She was the youngest and perhaps the bravest, having weathered society's ostracization when she and Dad married in 1947 and the inevitable questions they would get when she was on Dad's arm entering restaurants in Chicago where they first met: *"Are you together?"*

Mom downplayed the rejection and hatred they experienced, *"Oh, it was nothing."* But I know she internalized her pain, putting on a strong face and praying for healing at our family church to help her cope. In Eastern medicine, diseases of the lungs are said to represent grief. Mom certainly had her share.

Yet even throughout Dad's illness, Mom said, *"Saunders and I are very blessed, and God has been gracious to us, for which we give thanks."* When Dad played his last physical notes, his skin shining like the ebony-lacquered African cane he had been gifted by his brother, Kitsaun and I were at his bedside, our heads bent to hear any last words. Mom's wan body with a broken heart inside stood in their living room staring at the gray-green bay between San Rafael and Richmond, not wanting to face the end. The cool breeze gently drifted inside, the water through the trees glistened, and the cars on the San Rafael/Richmond Bridge sparkled.

Dad's breathing stopped and our weeping began. Kitsaun laid her head on Dad's chest, while I had a sense of being sent off into the unknown, like a child who lets go of the string of her red balloon, and it sails far away, out of sight.

———

AFTER DAD'S DEATH, MOM LIVED BY HERSELF in the house they had built. Her days were spent reading, praying, and writing in her journal. Kitsaun and I didn't know her private thoughts, but she became frail in the months after he died, so we knew her mourning was immense. There was an emptiness in their home. Later, I saw one of her journal entries:

Kitsaun and I spent more time with her, and at dinnertime, one of us took her food that we had cooked or picked up at Whole Foods. She sat at the dining room table, looking wistfully out at the bay, picking up forkfuls of steamed zucchini and small bites of baked salmon. Stories about the children's lives brightened her mood, and visits from them made her laugh from her belly.

Mom was always the person I told my life's concerns to. After work, I would tell her about the shenanigans at the office or where the band was on tour and when I might go meet them. She listened intently and gave me advice when appropriate. *"Remember to let go of the small irritations, Deb. Don't be so focused on perfection."* Mom often told me I worried too much.

Without Dad in their house, Kitsaun and I knew Mom was lonely. After all, she and Dad were married for fifty-three years. Their lives, so different outwardly, were perfectly melded together. I ached not having them together interacting with us with their overarching care and love. Dad's death was the gravest loss of Mom's life. Each day her soft face grew thinner and more haggard, and she looked physically weak. She was also diagnosed with emphysema, even though she had never smoked.

The disease did not prevent her from being her vibrant, witty, unconditional self, and giving tender love to all of us. Nevertheless, I called Ginette, the same woman who helped care for Dad, and asked her to begin caring for Mom. Her sweet spirit made Mom smile. They prayed together and discussed Scriptures, which bolstered them both. The children and I ran between our two houses to check on Mom and take her groceries, our dogs tagging along barking with joy.

Mom's pulmonologist prescribed oxygen therapy to aid her respiratory system and help her breathe easier. Mom didn't like taking the tank out in public, as the clicking sound it made drew unwanted attention to her disease, so she kept a tank next to her bed and used it at night. When

Mom no longer felt up to attending church services, she invited as many family members as possible to her house on Sunday afternoons. Cousins Emelda and Steve, and their children Ulysses and Kelli came, and cousins Sebastian and Kim, too. Mom sat in her chair with all of us crowded around her. We bantered about golfer Tiger Woods, whom Mom adored watching, and tennis greats Serena and Venus. We all laughed as we told stories about our dogs escaping from the yard and having to drive around the neighborhood searching for them.

She didn't feel up to cooking, so everyone brought something to share: baked chicken, spinach or greens, creamy polenta, apple pie, and vanilla ice cream bars covered in chocolate.

"*What was today's sermon?*" Mom asked.

"*Pastor preached that the miracle is that God works through ordinary circumstances to draw us close to Him. Our life journeys are a constant miracle from God,*" Emelda explained. Mom smiled.

She was happy to see everyone but tired easily and sat with her head against the back of her chair as we washed dishes and tidied up.

In fall 2005, Salvador left college and took his Salvador Santana Band on the road to clubs around the country and sometimes opened for Santana. He had been on the road since a young boy and knew how to conduct himself, make set lists, and offer his best to the audience. Stella was nearing her graduation from Pepperdine, and Angelica was in high school. I had been on a book tour, charmed by the people I met who had read *Space Between the Stars*. When I returned, I ran to Mom's house, breathless to share my experiences.

Mom talked as if she had settled her struggle with life's injustices and disappointments. "*I am willing to go when God calls me,*" she told me.

"*Don't say that, Mom,*" I begged. "*I want you to be at peace, but we have more fun trips to take all together, and you must teach us how to make your salmon patties. So many people at my book events asked about you.*" She smiled wanly but didn't comfort me in my distress at her words of resignation.

Then in January 2006, she called me. "*Deb, can you take me to the doctor? I can't seem to get rid of this cold.*" Her voice was raspy, and I heard a rattle as she spoke.

"Of course, Mom. I'll be right up." I drove out of my driveway and around the street to hers.

She held onto my arm as we walked from my car to the doctor's office; her body was frail. We sat with her pulmonologist for what we thought would be an examination ending with a prescription of antibiotics for bronchitis. Instead, the doctor said, *"If she were my mother, I would take her right to the hospital."*

"Mom, I think we should do as Dr. Livnat said." She was too weak to disagree. On the short drive to Marin General, I felt as though I was skidding down the side of a steep mountain, hitting every sharp crag and tree stump, my skin being cut and bruised.

That day was the beginning of my Zen experience with my darling mother's last five months on earth. With her pale skin, high cheekbones, light hazel eyes, and thin body, she looked like the mother she had always been, but her breath was fading.

She was admitted to room 2134 at Marin General Hospital. I sat beside her bed as she breathed into a nebulizer to help clear her bronchitis. I was alone with Mom's illness, anguishing over her life and fearing her death. I was lost.

When Dad's body was shutting down, I felt guilty for wanting the process to end so that he could be free from his suffering. With Mom, I was present with every change in her body, grateful for her acceptance to be willing to go *"when God called her,"* even though I wasn't.

Dr. Livnat called me into the hallway. *"Your mother could live a year, two years, or die tomorrow. She is at the end stage of her disease."* Any lingering idea I had of control was stripped away. I listened closely to each of his statements, struggling to accept the truth, hardly able to breathe myself. My eyes filled with tears. There was great anguish in my heart that this mother—who loved me so, who taught me to feel God and honor Spirit and the value of truth and hard work—would leave this earthly plane. I cherished the familial love and gentle sharing of our time together.

No push or pull, Mom and I just looked into each other's eyes with knowing and peace that we would go through it together. It was a time to learn and experience life changing into a more radiant form. Weakness became strength. All changed inside of me. It was all love.

Kitsaun arrived, and Mom seemed to be sleeping, so I drove home, where Angelica was waiting. Salvador was in the home studio rehearsing with his band in preparation to take them on the road with his dad, and Stella was in Los Angeles. Salvador didn't understand that Mom's days were waning and followed his dad's lead to go on tour.

During the three days Mom stayed at Marin General that January, I sat in her room with Josh Baran's *365 Nirvana Here and Now*, reading my way into myself. My other companions of self-discovery were Hafiz, T.S. Eliot, Alice Walker, Henry David Thoreau, and Sylvia Boorstein. There was an exquisite stillness in Mom's sleeping, in our togetherness. She was teaching me something important about dying.

Mom offered me an unspoken wisdom about living, too. I didn't understand it all because I was still working as hard as I could to keep my family, business, and nonprofit foundation in order. She was letting go, and with deliberate, conscious awareness, I began letting go as well.

Kitsaun and I brought her back home and talked about her wishes as we watched her body get weaker from the cruelty of emphysema. We had no idea how deeply she was suffering; emphysema was once described to me as "trying to breathe through a tiny red plastic coffee straw."

She wrote Carlos and me a thank you card: "*This past year, your family has helped me in ways you don't realize. Remember to love the journey and don't miss the view. Take care of your three angels.*"

In March of 2006, Mom told me again that she was at peace. "*God can take me anytime.*" She wrote out Bible verses and aphorisms that gave her strength and hope: "*Pain is not a flower; pain is a root, and its work is underground. . .*" from "Gardenias" by Paul Monette. Or she wrote her own words: "*My intention is to be healthy, to breathe freely at all times, and to be comfortable walking.*"

Two months later, her friend and caregiver, Ginette, arrived to help her with breakfast, and she found Mom unconscious. Ginette called me, and I ran to Mom's house just as the paramedics arrived.

They couldn't revive Mom and lifted her into the ambulance on a gurney. I climbed in too, bouncing in the worn leather passenger seat, watching Mom's head roll from side to side as the paramedic stuck an IV in her thin arm, and my mother's red blood spurted onto the floor. There was something incredibly human and surrendering watching Mom's blood spill and not being able to stop it, or even to cradle her body. I still didn't know that her sweet life was nearly over.

That afternoon, with Kitsaun, Stella, and Angelica around the bed, Mom regained consciousness for an hour. She looked around at her daughters and granddaughters, along with cousin Emelda and my friends Lynn and Ellen, and said, *"You all go home; I'm going home."*

One by one, each of us leaned over the bed and hugged her slim frame and kissed her cheeks as she patted our arms. We stood with tears in our eyes, like abandoned children. I draped my body across the bed and rubbed her hand.

We watched her body labor to let go of this dimension of existence, and I replayed mental videos of conversations, hugs, and laughter—of Mom eating her nightly ice cream bar while she watched reruns of *The Waltons*; of her arms holding Salvador as a chubby baby; of her coloring with Stella or laying on her bed reading a nighttime story when I came home from class at Dominican University; and of Mom telling me how she'd laughed at Angelica's stories as they drove over Wolfe Grade together after Angelica's day at preschool.

I thought of Mom as a young woman dating and marrying Dad, not even being allowed to legally take his name because interracial marriage was illegal in California, so I was born Deborah King to Jo Frances Willis. She never exalted herself for being so brave and revolutionary. To Mom, it was simply love. But I knew.

Early the next morning, I cut a dozen roses from our garden and arrived at the hospital, where I cleaned off the tray over her bed, washed her unmoving face with a warm, wet washcloth, and played Salvador's music in hopes that she could hear her grandson's hands on the piano keys.

I thought about those last words she spoke: *"You all go home; I'm going home."* Had she meant she was going to her house, where we eventually transported her? Or had she meant her heavenly home, where she knew she was destined? The great mystery of what we know at our time of death opened wide when she said those prophetic words.

Four days after she was admitted, we took her back home, and on May 20, 2006, Mom's sips of breath stopped. There was an immense void where her body had been, where her soul had sheltered.

———

I MISS MY MOTHER DEEPLY: her magnificent heart-opening smile, her gumption.

Mom's interest in every person she met was real—authentic to the bone. Dad often scolded her for talking to the scruffy, soiled man in the Montecito Shopping Center and giving him one-dollar bills; she didn't need to know his story, only that he was in need. She taught us so many truths, and the fact that she always preferred women dentists and doctors, politicians, and athletes, showed us early on that women are forces of nature to be admired and loved.

Her body may be gone, but the fire of her life continues to illuminate our hearts, the garden, the sky, our world.

Loving the Fire

I wish my mother had not died before I found my way
    through a burning forest, flames crawling up bark and
    branch, singeing my legs as I ran.
She would have feared for my life despite her faith in the Divine.
    She would have angered when people who were not strangers
    did not offer their hands
    to pull me from the astounding heat.

My trials would have been easier with her arms around me,
    as her womb had enfolded my beginning.
From her perch in the beyond, I felt her blessing,

and out of the ashes my courage rose,
*   like notes of violins, flutes, and cellos.*

I wish my mother had told me how she survived
*   the burning of her life.*
Looking upward, toward a patriarchal God in cumulus clouds,
*   she wore rose-colored glasses on her thin nose,*
*   porcelain skin radiant from her fire.*
My fears breathed in shadows outside my windows,
*   and doubts that I was enough to be loved*
*   were incinerated by clarinets and violas*
*   whose round full notes carry the refreshing wind of this new day.*

6

THE STUNNING MYSTERIES OF LIFE

THE WEEK BEFORE MOM'S DEATH, I attended an informational meeting at New College of California to consider applying for a Bachelor of Arts completion program. With *Space Between the Stars* out in the world, I felt compelled to continue living my authentic life. I wanted to complete the college education I had walked away from twice—the last time to join Carlos's life odyssey. The school sat in a row of funky buildings on Valencia Street in the Mission District. I walked into a classroom where the meeting was taking place, the desks and chairs a little worse for the wear and was given paperwork to fill out. The enrollment advisor explained there would be a prior learning component which meant I could receive credit for the business management at Santana and Dipti Nivas, and for my published memoir.

Carlos and Salvador flew home from Europe for two days to attend Mom's funeral. Salvador embraced me and then rolled up his sleeve to show me a tattoo of Mom's full name on his forearm: Jo Frances King, in a beautiful script. Carlos and I hugged and then he lay on our bed and watched TV. He didn't ask me how I felt or how I was coping, and I didn't dive into his arms for consolation. We didn't connect in comfort or pain.

Mom's going home service was at our family church in Oakland. We parked and walked up the three stone steps and through the wooden doors. Flower arrangements crowded the altar and on stands in front of Mom's casket. Her casket—her temporary home before going back to the earth. I felt breathless seeing the last place I could touch Mom's face. Our family and friends quietly wept as my cousin Pastor Ulysses Stephen King, Jr. delivered the eulogy. We had printed a message to Mom in the program:

We love you! You are a model of God's Peace and His Grace, His Love, and His Joy. Thank you for being his vessel of hope for our family. Your strength of character lives in us all.

I sat between my daughters, Salvador and Carlos beside us. I was a cloud of heartbreak in the farewell ceremony, a vapor in the pew. Somehow, we all got through the day comforting each other.

Speaking the words of my book at each event had been my "coming out" as Deborah in the world. I had minimized Carlos's infidelity in my memoir, but painful betrayals surfaced in my memories. When Salvador and Carlos flew back to Europe, I didn't trust Carlos would be faithful to me, and I no longer wanted to think about the possibility of other women in his life. I had pruned my life branches too short for me to blossom and admitted to myself that Carlos and I were broken and most likely could not be repaired. I didn't yet know how to exit the marriage without upset-ting our family, but I thought about it almost daily.

I completed staff performance evaluations at Santana Management and was finishing applications for Angelica to travel to Florence in the summer to participate in an Italian language program. She was fifteen and ready to be in Italy with her friend in a homestay. All the plans I made were coming to fruition, but Mom was no longer with me.

Alberto Villoldo, PhD, wrote in the article "Homo Luminous": "*We are constantly challenged to face little deaths in our lives: who we once were, a rela-tionship ending, loss of a loved one, a career, a cherished time in our lives. During transitions, we have time to reinvent ourselves. When we don't, a deadening hap-pens. That deadening causes us to age instead of becoming the sage. If we go through these little deaths consciously, they become opportunities for new life. If we have the prerequisite courage, instead of being wounded by transitions, we become inspired by them. How we respond to adversity turns us into courageous beings."*

One day, I drove to Calistoga and sat in a tub of healing clay as a therapist massaged the tender loss out of my body. Most days, I walked the hills above our home and watched early morning fog lift off the bay. I began to feel a restful calm in my body and sent Angelica off to Italy and Stella back to Los Angeles.

Alone, I sat at the pond between two empty houses: ours and Mom and Dad's. In that time of loss, I was not lonely but pensive and reflective of the stunning mysteries of life. I sat in the aura of Mom's and Dad's spirits hovering over me.

———

In mid-July, I arrived at the San Francisco airport three hours before my departure to join Angelica in Italy. Mothers pulled wiggling children along by their hands as passengers rolled suitcases across the marble floor of the international terminal. I joined the line for Flight 455 to Frankfurt, the stopover for my flight to Florence, Italy.

The moment I placed my ticket on the Lufthansa counter, I had a premonition that something wasn't right. The ticket agent flipped the pages of my passport, turning from my photo to the back.

"Did you add extra pages to your passport?" she asked.

"No," I said.

Her forehead creased with lines, and she said in a soft voice, *"I'm sorry. Your passport is expired. You can go to that counter there and reschedule your travel."* As she pointed, my eyes followed her fingers to see the adjoining counter.

I had traveled by myself to Europe, Japan, South America, and Australia for more than thirty years. My documents had always been in order and my passport current. I was shocked that I had not checked my passport, but I also knew I had been focused on Mom and the children. I calmly thanked the agent, rolled my suitcase past the suggested reservation counter, and sat down in a plastic molded chair in front of the sky-high windows facing the street. Surprise and disbelief filled me. I telephoned my office, asking for help, then I sat, reflecting on the reason I was in this predicament.

After Mom's memorial service, someone told me I was an orphan in this world. In that vulnerable moment with my expired passport, those words sank in. I wondered whether I could make the trip to meet my daughter and her friend in Florence.

Mom hadn't traveled with our family in three years, but I had always known where she was; my inner compass aligned with her prayers for me. She and Dad had been in Florence with us in 1988, the year before Angelica was born—eating pasta, shopping for shoes, and laughing as we watched Salvador and Stella gaze at the magnificence of Michelangelo's *David*. Now, waiting for my friend to arrive at the airport to pick me up, I felt the absence of my mother as my physical anchor, as though I had no solid ground beneath my feet, and I was floating along with her soul.

Through the extreme kindness of our travel agent and my office staff, I had a new passport in only three and a half hours. The following day, I traveled from San Francisco's Pacific Coast to Italy's Tuscan clay, listening to my collection of music, which included Salvador's composition, "Dear Lord"—the song I played for Mom in her hospital room—his mature, singular voice singing over his chords on the piano.

The front doors of the Plaza Hotel Lucchesi opened onto the river Arno, and each time I crossed the threshold, I felt renewal. My room had a small balcony that faced the Duomo, Brunelleschi's Cathedral of Saint Maria del Fiore. I sat on a small iron chair, admiring the brick dome and golden ball atop the fifteenth-century masterpiece. Nothing in America had this antiquity or beauty. Angelica was thriving studying Italian every day in a local institute, living with an Italian family. I walked past groves of olive trees up a steep road to reach Chiesa di San Miniato al Monte, the eleventh-century chapel whose simple wooden doors led to rustic hand-painted crosses and a golden altar.

Beneath a frescoed cupola, I lit a waxy votive candle and whispered a prayer to Mom's soul; I remembered her body before the undertaker came, her shoulders curved slightly forward as if to fold her body into a neat envelope of everlasting life. Kitsaun and I had laid our hands upon her heart, like a postage stamp to send her body back to God. She looked like a paper doll in her silky, flowered pajamas, not breathing—a petite shell of the warrior she once was—a shattering image to hold.

In the filtered sunlight of the church, the smoke rising from the extinguished match drifted upward, and I felt the smallness of crossing continents and oceans.

Every morning the skies were blue and clear over the Tuscan hills; swallows and doves danced outside my terrace; cathedral bells chimed. All throughout Florence, I searched for human connections and clues of spiritual essence. I saw myself in the rakish ferry captain; the nuns scooting quietly through churches; the skilled sculptor; the mother cuddling the chubby, crying baby; and the waiter pouring my *agua natural*.

We walked different roads, but the lessons were the same. Life was a daily renaissance with social and emotional upheaval, and the need to adjust and adapt, and be transformed by the uncomfortable nuances of death.

Sitting in my favorite cafe, the Golden View Open Bar, I watched tourists through the enormous windows open to the Arno as they crowded the Ponte Vecchio. I remembered the single tear that slid down Mom's cheek in the emergency room. Had she been in physical pain? Or was she frustrated that we had not let her fly off into infinity but instead had rushed her to the hospital with the ambulance's blaring siren destroying her peace?

The orange blaze of the setting sun reflected in the river cradled my spirit. I knew in my soul that in her death, Mom was able to fully breathe again, and she was commandeering Dad and her sisters in heaven, just as she had gathered the family around her dining room table on Sunday afternoons when she would tell stories about each of us, give Dad's face a loving pat, squeeze Angelica's cheeks, tell Stella how smart she was as she assembled new pots and pans, and measure Salvador's height against the years of pencil marks on the wall.

My mother, the goddess of compassion, with her quick words of truth, caressed my face with her soft hands in the Tuscan breeze. She understood that I needed to write new chapters in my life.

ARTISTS FOR A NEW SOUTH AFRICA

WITH MOM GONE THE EMPTINESS IN MY LIFE WAS PALPABLE. I waited for her phone call—to run up to her house—and had to remind myself she was an ancestor now, on another plane of existence. I still had book signings and flew to Seattle to read at Elliott Bay Book Company. Kitsaun accompanied me to the shadow of Mt. Rainier, exquisitely rising behind the city, with puffs of fog drifting around the mouth of the crater. We continued to Portland, New York, and Boston, each reading a glowing exchange between my heart and the audience.

Back home in California, Sharon Gelman, executive director of Artists for a New South Africa, the Los Angeles-based nonprofit, hosted a reading for me at Creative Artists Agency, the talent agency that represented Carlos. So many of our industry friends attended the festive event. I wore a sleeveless white silk sheath with silver embroidery and was shivering in the air conditioning, or was it my nerves? Sharon curated the program: Carlos and Salvador performed first, then Angelica read her poem "SK Blues," printed in the back pages of *Space Between the Stars*, and finally, I read excerpts from my memoir. Stella sat in the front row beside

ANSA board members Samuel L. Jackson and LaTanya Richardson Jackson; George, Ann, and Mayan Lopez; Herbie and Gigi Hancock; and our attorneys and booking agents. I felt loved by these friends—validated, celebrated, and humbled.

Months later, ANSA hosted Archbishop Desmond Tutu's visit to Los Angeles, and Carlos and I were invited to lunch with our friends. The archbishop walked into the restaurant at the Peninsula Hotel in Beverly Hills carrying a bright blue plastic donut in his arm, the comforting pillow given to mothers after childbirth, which he was using in his recovery from prostate surgery. He greeted us with bubbles of laughter and joy, and it was as if hundreds of champagne bottles had been uncorked.

"Hello, dear ones," he said to Carlos and me as we sat down to discuss his new role as honorary chair of the Amandla AIDS Fund, which was started with the proceeds from Santana's *Shaman* summer tour. We gratefully supported ANSA in their continued work in South Africa to fight HIV/AIDS.

We first met the archbishop in 2000 when he and his wife, Leah, came to California as part of a speaking tour to thank Americans for supporting sanctions against South Africa and fighting to abolish apartheid. Carlos and I hosted a dinner at our home before the archbishop's speaking engagement at the Marin Civic Center, and we considered the archbishop and his wife beloved friends from the moment we met.

During our Los Angeles luncheon, the Arch, as we all called him, spoke about how South Africa would be better served through the wisdom of women leaders, and he whispered with a rather roguish look on his face, *"I counseled President Nelson Mandela to stop shacking up with Graça Machel . . . and get married."* He giggled at his own hubris.

In the Arch's presence, I was filled with awe and respect for his sage spiritual and political voice in our world. Our meal together gave me a taste of his mind and the vast range of his abilities to move from global concerns to family issues.

The Arch invited ANSA board members and friends to South Africa to attend a celebration for his 75th birthday, which would be held in October 2006. A flurry of activity ensued as twenty-five people—including our family—signed on to make the journey to South Africa to visit the programs and services supported by ANSA.

It would be a great honor to join this group of activists, but the pilgrimage was just a few months after Mom's death. I was still grieving my way through each day, stumbling along, and praying each morning for a small breath of wisdom in my meditation. The importance of visiting the land of Mandela, Tutu, and the freedom fighters who had published writings, attended trials, lost countless loved ones, and put their lives at risk to resist and dismantle forty-six years of white minority government was not something I could miss. Traveling with family would be a comfort, although Stella decided to stay home and not disrupt her junior year at Pepperdine.

Our delegation, which traveled from Los Angeles, New York, and Washington, DC, was cared for and herded by ANSA staff. Sharon led our group, which included actress Alfre Woodard and her writer-producer husband, Roderick Spencer; LaTanya Richardson Jackson and her daughter, Zoë; actress CCH Pounder and her art-curator husband, Boubacar Kone; actress and youngest ANSA board member, Jurnee Smollett; my sister, Kitsaun, and her partner, Gregory Robinson. Carlos and Salvador were on tour and joined us in DC after three weeks of concerts.

Our plane touched down on the continent in Senegal at midnight. Traces of sultry air floated into the cabin as new passengers boarded the plane, and I marveled that I was in Africa for the first time in my life. In the layer of cells beneath my skin, I transitioned from an American to feeling like a citizen of the place civilization was born. A purple black sky beckoned through the small airplane window, and I thought of my ancestry that began on African soil. The air sifting through the open airplane door carried the sweet scent of jasmine blossoms, and I remembered what Nelson Mandela wrote in *Long Walk to Freedom*: "*The air of one's home always smells sweet after one has been away.*"

We began our trip in Cape Town at the Mount Nelson Hotel, with the view from our room looking out at the majestic cliffs of Table Mountain. Cape Town was a beautiful coastal city, not unlike San Francisco or Sydney, with curving streets, boutiques, and parks. In the cool October wind, palm trees swayed above paths that skirted the hotel grounds, and I could see the entrance lit with opulent crystal chandeliers. Inside our room, thick brocade curtains hung from black rods with silver pinecone finials. Pressed lilies and chrysanthemums with hand-drawn stems were suspended in frames on walls covered in gilded wallpaper.

The ghosts of apartheid hovered within this luxuriant lodging, making me hyper aware of the privilege of each person in our group and uncomfortable with my own affluence in contrast to the scenes of oppression and hardship all around. Through the window, I saw women wearing thin coats over simple dresses disembarking from buses to walk to their work, domestic, and factory jobs. It had only been fourteen years since apartheid and institutionalized segregation had ended, along with the violence inflicted on the Black populace by Afrikaners.

We traveled by private bus, and each time we boarded, we called out the number Sharon had assigned to us to ensure no one was left behind at the hotel. I was number fifteen, the middle of the group of activists.

On our first morning, we were to visit the Philani Child Health and Nutrition Project in Khayelitsha, a project dear to the Arch. Carlos said, *"I'm going to stay at the hotel."* I was disappointed but accepted that the pattern of us being apart would continue on this once-in-a-lifetime journey.

In Khayelitsha township, a few miles north of our hotel, we passed tin-roofed shacks with cardboard walls, roofs covered with plastic garbage bags held down by buckets, broken strollers, and cement blocks. Kerosene stoves and bonfires burned in the streets emitting a choking smoke. Khayelitsha was where Black Cape Town families were forced to settle in the early 1980s—outcasts on their own land since 1652.

In a compound composed of four simple cement buildings with schoolrooms and a handicraft shop, Philani had meeting areas where mothers were educated in protecting their children's health and preventing malnutrition and were taught skills for income-generating projects to further their economic independence. I smiled at children laughing and shrieking as they chased each other over the play structures. Salvador went onto the playground and pushed the children on tire swings and slapped high fives on the palms of boys running past him.

ANSA's staff had distributed binders to each delegate about ANSA's work with AIDS Foundation South Africa and Ingwavuma Orphan Care. ANSA had a deep respect for Indigenous knowledge, so rather than imposing American systems on the agencies it worked with, it supported the efforts of local community organizations and walked softly under the guidance of local leaders and grassroots workers. There was a collaboration of roles and implementation of programs to combat HIV/AIDS, assist children orphaned by the disease, advance human and civil rights, educate and empower youth, and build bonds between the two nations through arts, culture, and a shared pursuit of social justice.

Our delegation had a tightly scheduled eight-day sojourn. On the second morning in Cape Town, our dear friend Ahmed Kathrada ("Kathy")—a veteran of the South African liberation struggle, one of the famous African National Congress (ANC) leaders imprisoned after the Rivonia Trial and a prisoner on Robben Island in Pollsmoor Maximum Security Prison—took us on a tour of Robben Island.

I had first met Kathy at his book signing at Hue-Man Bookstore (now known as Huemanbooks) in Harlem, where he presented his extraordinary book *Memoirs* to those of us sitting in folding chairs in the notable bookstore. Kathy's personal sacrifices in the anti-apartheid struggle—which culminated in his incarceration—were only more impressive to me when I learned that while imprisoned at Robben Island, he earned a bachelor's degree in history and criminology and a second bachelor's degree in African politics and library science. He also received honors in history and African studies.

Over tea in the front windows of Hue-Man, my heart moved into Kathy's world. He said, *"We could see the African penguins swimming about and catching fish in the seas. Their natural lives buoyed my spirits."* Now I was here on Robben Island with Kathy, listening intently as he shared his personal stories of being incarcerated there for eighteen years with Nelson Mandela.

Our group walked inside cement cells, where prisoners were kept fourteen hours a day with only a thin woolen mat to sit and sleep on, and warders who constantly harassed and abused them. After fourteen years, the prisoners finally received cots to sleep on. Angelica, sixteen years old, said, *"They were without beds almost my entire life."*

As we approached Mandela's cell, Kathy lifted the key into the air. "*Who wants to open the door?*" Voices began calling out, "*Sal! Sal!*" Our twenty-three-year-old son gingerly took the rusted metal key from Kathy's hand and attempted to turn the lock. After two tries, the paint-chipped-barred door opened. We cheered as Salvador pushed open the prison door that had held Mandela captive and allowed us to stand in the hallowed space.

None of us uttered a word as we took turns standing inside the cell imagining ourselves imprisoned in those bleak surroundings. Mandela said the cell gave him the opportunity to meditate on his life, his feelings, and his thoughts. Looking out of the small window high up in the wall, I experienced the silence that he and the other prisoners lived with day after day.

Kathy explained, without rancor, that the maniacal apartheid system differentiated "Coloureds" (people of Indian descent or mixed-race) from Blacks. "*The Black prisoners were not allowed to wear long pants or socks, were not given bread, and were rationed only one and one-half teaspoons of sugar each day. My group, the Coloureds and Indians, was given long pants and socks and bread and two teaspoons of sugar each day.*"

Lights in the cells were kept on twenty-four hours a day, showers were freezing-cold seawater, prisoners were not allowed to read after the required hour for sleep, and they were only allowed to write and receive letters once every six months, and only of 500 words or less, all heavily censored. They were forced to work at the bright white lime quarry under the strong Southern sun without any protective eye covering, which was why Mandela's eyesight was so poor when he was freed. Even when a lawyer could visit, the warder would control their conversation so that only family matters could be discussed.

While Kathy explained the discriminatory acts and restrictions placed on these heroes of South African freedom, I reflected on people's ability to torture others with brutal, inhumane practices.

At their Rivonia Trial, Mandela spoke for four hours and ended with these famous words, "*I have fought against white domination . . . for which I am prepared to die.*" In his speech, Mandela passionately spoke of the ways apartheid had stripped Africans of dignity, destroyed their family life, and shredded their society. The men were all prepared for execution, but they were given life sentences in prison and were flown to Robben Island in the middle of the night—not to see a child again for twelve years.

At the end of our tour of Robben Island, Kathy led us to the shore where hundreds of charming seabirds stood on rocks shaking their tails and nodding their heads as if in greeting. Waddling back and forth, they looked so harmless and cute, and I felt how much joy these birds must have given the prisoners.

Disembarking from the Robben Island ferry, we boarded our bus quietly, feeling somber and melancholy after standing in Nelson Mandela's cell and ingesting statistics about their years of incarceration. Carlos moved to the front of the bus and inserted a CD in the console. The strains of Sam Cooke singing "A Change Is Gonna Come" filtered through the speakers, and a collective cry spread through the bus. The violins and horns sang a plaintive melody, and Alfre climbed onto Roderick's lap, hugging him tightly. Jurnee's eyes filled with tears. Kitsaun and Gregory slow danced in the aisle of the rocking bus. All of us felt the significance of the lyrics. . . .

"I was born by a river, in a little tent,
Oh, and just like the river, I've been running ever since.
It's been a long, a long time coming,
but I know a change gonna come . . ."

Although the song brought other couples together to comfort each other, Carlos stayed on the step by the driver, facing forward looking out the window, and I remained in my seat a few rows back, watching the road scatter under the wheels of the bus, while pieces of my heart were being crushed in the pain of loneliness. I didn't feel close enough to my husband to let my guard down and embrace him, and he didn't turn and pull me to him. Distance was our reality.

THE NEXT DAY, WE FLEW TO JOHANNESBURG, a city of fences—around every neighborhood, family compound, and throughout the downtown. Walls and barbed wire kept people apart from each other. We were to be given a tour of Constitution Hill by the poetic genius Justice Albie Sachs. Sachs's career in human rights activism began at the age of seventeen, and the bulk of his work involved defending people charged under racist statutes and repressive security laws. Many faced the death sentence.

Albie was under constant surveillance by the security police; he was subjected to banning orders restricting his movement and eventually was placed in solitary confinement without trial for two prolonged periods. In 1988, while he was in Mozambique, South African security agents hid a bomb in his car. When he opened the door, the explosion nearly ended his life. He lost his right arm and sight in one eye.

A genuine hero in the anti-apartheid movement, Albie stood outside our bus, waving as we pulled up. His smile was open and luminous as each person stepped down from the bus. "*Deborah!*" he exclaimed. "*Welcome to the Constitution Court.*"

I walked into his embrace, feeling awe: "*Thank you, Albie.*" He led us up the Great African Steps to the court, the front of the building showcasing the words "Constitutional Court," written in rainbow colors and in all eleven official languages spoken in South Africa.

The tower of light over the Awaiting Trial Block building, and the thin, river-like window that ran along the brick wall to the left of the justices' bench, told a story. "*It reminds the judges to remain pious, to see who people are without color or gender, and to remember that they are there to serve the people,*" he said.

The Man Who Sang and the Woman Who Kept Silent by Judith Mason hung in the walkway to the front doors of the court. Albie explained that the triptych depicts a dress, made from bits of blue plastic, being torn at by a predatory animal. The artist had been listening to the Truth and Reconciliation Commission hearings on the radio and heard the story of Phila Ndwandwe, an MK fighter in the ANC, the political party known for its opposition, often violent, to apartheid. She was abducted and tortured for ten days to pressure her into becoming an informant. When she still refused, the Apartheid police assassinated her. She was found naked in a shallow grave, covered only with a small piece of blue plastic over her private parts. In the radio interview, the policeman who shot her in the head said, "*She was brave. Very brave.*" She had been a warrior who had refused to bow to apartheid.

Mason decided to make the woman a dress to clothe her in her death. Alfre read the inscription beside the artwork, her voice quivering with emotion, and I imagined seeing the naked woman shivering as she hid, wondering about her children and her husband, and if she would survive. It was important for me to allow the experiences I was learning about to enter my heart; I didn't want to intellectualize South Africa's history, as if I was observing something long gone. The air in Johannesburg still carried the cries of those killed in the atrocities of apartheid.

Alfre's voice broke as she read the final words, "*Sister, a plastic bag may not be the whole armor of God, but you were wrestling with flesh and blood, and against powers, against the rulers of darkness. . .*" Alfre lifted her head high, and we stood quietly for a few moments, honoring Phila Ndwandwe and thousands more like her.

We boarded our bus and Albie waved goodbye, eager to return to his wife, Vanessa September, who was due to deliver their baby any hour. We toured Soweto, where 4 million people of color lived, led by an energetic, soft-spoken freedom fighter named Rita.

Before I came to South Africa, Soweto was a beautiful-sounding name spoken in conversations about apartheid and sung with plaintive voices in songs about police shootings and demonstrations. Driving into the township, we saw taxi ranks, small houses, and dirt roads off the main thoroughfare. We entered the Regina Mundi Catholic Church, where citizens sought refuge and hid beneath pews when members of the security forces chased them down and shot at them. People on the streets smiled and waved their arms at us with love; I wondered how they could be so open and trusting after all they endured.

We were driven down Vilakazi Street—past the Arch and Leah Tutu's house, then past Mandela's former house—my senses attuned to the historical meetings that had clandestinely taken place. That the Tutu family still lived in the community was a profound example of their humility and commitment to the ideals of freedom, rather than the gain of personal riches.

An extraordinary two hours of our journey occurred the next morning when our delegation traveled to the Nelson Mandela Foundation in Johannesburg. We were granted an audience with the former anti-apartheid leader and president of South Africa, an honor each of us excitedly anticipated. Alfre, Roderick, CCH Pounder, LaTanya, and Sam had all met Mr. Mandela before, but that didn't dampen their joy.

I had seen Mandela only from a great distance, standing on centerfield of the Oakland Coliseum on June 30, 1990, when he appeared to speak of his triumph. I was one of 60,000 supporters cheering every word. Now there were just thirty of us on this hallowed pilgrimage.

As we waited for Mr. Mandela to arrive in the small auditorium, my father came to mind. My father walked like an African king with long strides, arms swinging close to his body, his hips loose. It was his high waist and derriere like a shelf, his thin calves, and long feet with flesh-colored soles bleeding into the black of his ankles that belonged to my unknown ancestors. His posture and the cadence of his tenor voice were elegant. He never hurried his conversation or anyone else's but listened to it all with the dignity of a tribal chief.

In the auditorium, we were surrounded by framed photographs of monumental historic moments on the walls: Mandela in 1964, broad shouldered and young; Winnie Mandela and their two daughters standing outside the courthouse at the Rivonia Trial sentencing. I was astounded to see that Mandela's prison records contained more than 45,000 artifacts. An entire apartheid government could barely accommodate his profound writings or track his studious recordings of each day's thoughts and plans. This beautiful brick building with picture windows—new, modern, and immaculately clean—is what the former president of South Africa, who was long imprisoned in a cell smaller than this building's bathroom, deserved.

Mr. Mandela entered the auditorium smiling, holding a white cane and leaning on the arm of Ms. Zelda la Grange, his spokesperson and personal assistant. Here he was in the flesh—the world leader whose hunger for freedom helped liberate South Africa. I could not say it was a dream come true because I had never expected I would have an audience with him. I was content just being alive to witness the impact that his vision, fearlessness, and tenacity had on our world.

Interacting with our delegation, Mr. Mandela was a lighthearted sharp-shooter, asking each of us questions and shaking our hands. He listened to each of our answers, and we laughed and savored his friendliness. I noticed a twinkle in his eye, one remarkably similar to the light in Kathy's eyes, and a thought flashed through my mind about the conditions these men had endured. Because of my own devotion to silence through meditation, I wondered if the imposed solitude of prison gave them an inner depth of relationship with "self" that allowed this inner joy.

I had written a card to give to Mr. Mandela and misspelled Madiba, his traditional Xhosa clan name. A clan name is much more important than a surname as it refers to the ancestor from which a person is descended. Madiba was the name of a Thembu chief who ruled in the Transkei in the 18th century. It is considered very polite to use someone's clan name, and I had wanted to be respectful.

As a wise teacher, he corrected my spelling error. *"There is no 'n' in Madiba,"* he said, pointing at my handwriting on the envelope while craning his neck to look at me with kindness. I felt like a schoolchild beside the statesman.

Salvador and Angelica stood behind Mr. Mandela's chair, smiling for photographs and hanging onto each word he spoke.

"So, who proposed to whom?" he asked, looking from Carlos to me. Such a pointed, unusual question, like an arrow shot directly at the estrangement I felt from my husband.

Mandela laughed, everyone in the delegation laughed, and I smiled. *"He did,"* I answered. Carlos's smile seemed forced, but no one knew what I did—our marriage was deeply strained; we were on the outskirts of our community of two.

When Alfre and Roderick took their turn beside Mandela, Alfre asked, *"May I give you a kiss?"* and Mandela answered, *"Certainly,"* and threw his head back to laugh.

When our time with the great leader was ending, Mandela said, *"Please give my regards to the Americans,"* as though our delegation represented an entire country as he so regally did.

My body was afloat from being in Mandela's presence, a joy that I remembered from the 1990s when I watched him on the evening news, dancing the *toyi-toyi*—a marching side-to-side hop, with his arms bent at the elbows. I always loved seeing him move with the people in a freedom dance. This liberation dance signified South Africans' solidarity and strength, and it echoed the elegant movement of my own father.

The evening of the Arch's birthday celebration, our delegation was treated like royalty in the festivities. Sam and LaTanya walked the red carpet to flashing bulbs. Alfre glowed in a full-length lavender gown beside Roderick. Jurnee joined Angelica and Salvador at our table as Johnny Clegg took the stage singing "Asimbonanga," all of us swaying to the victory song. President Mandela stood and danced, his smile resplendent. I celebrated the auspiciousness of the night.

The last two days of our journey took us four hours north of Durban in the province of KwaZulu-Natal. This destination was the ultimate purpose of our journey—to visit families supported by ANSA's Amandla AIDS Fund through the service of Ingwavuma Orphan Care. We drove ninety minutes from our hotel to an area where 42 percent of the population was living with HIV/AIDS. At the Nsongweni Primary School, children received their education in buildings without electricity or water supply, and with few resources. A staff of seven taught 213 pupils between the ages of five and nineteen. Twenty-three were orphans. We walked to the garden where the children grew vegetables to feed the students and their families. Dr. Ann Dean, head of the program, gave us background about Ingwavuma. *"It's not a village or town but a wide, dispersed area. The population we're trying to cover is 100,000, and 59 percent are under nineteen years of age. Nearly half the families have no income."* Digesting this information, ANSA board members thanked the workers and their families for allowing us, through our donations, to be of service in the AIDS pandemic.

LaTanya is a stunningly beautiful woman with arms wide enough to enfold everyone she meets and a mind wise enough to play notable character roles and direct television series and plays. She stood and said, *"I'm LaTanya Jackson, ANSA board member, and I'm just here to love you and let you love me."*

Sam stood beside her. *"I'm Sam Jackson, ANSA mascot."* Laughter sparked around the room, and he continued, *"And I just want to say thanks for letting us come and hang out with you today. I hope you get as much from us as we get from you."*

We were driven into the bush to meet families supported by ANSA's funding. We met Gogo (Grandmother) Mabandlase, whose five sons had died from AIDS, and her remaining child, a daughter, was in Durban looking for work. Surrounded by her eight grandchildren, holding a baby in her arms, Gogo spoke to us in Zulu through an interpreter: *"The assistance we get from the government falls far short of what we need. I am stranded and have nothing. I am taking care of all these children with no one to help me."*

Salvador, Angelica, and Carlos carried sacks of rice and beans, cans of vegetables, and other staples into the family's unlit, single story, completely empty storeroom while I knelt by Gogo, holding her hand.

Her smile was pure sunlight. *"I'm delighted and moved by your spirit of generosity,"* she said through the translator. *"I have been feeling so alone, but now I feel a part of a larger human family."* She squeezed my hand, and I brought her hand to my face and kissed her fingers. Gogo enchanted us with her big love, and I will never forget her sitting on a thin blanket surrounded by her grandbabies.

Zulu children sang and danced for us—a feeling of spiritual blessing through their words and song. We were tired from our rigorous travel schedule, but we met for a final dinner together at the Pongola Game Reserve. The air was warm and scented with dust touched by the hooves of elephants and zebras. The dining room chefs and servers pulled Carlos and Sam onto the floor to dance while we all clapped.

Early the next morning, our family climbed into a van for our journey back to Durban Airport to fly back to Johannesburg, then to Washington, DC, and, finally home to California. The staff of our small lodge formed a circle and sang a farewell song as we drove away.

My heart carried the sky inside me, and the words of Tutu, Albie, and Mandela. I was so grateful to have borne witness to the lives of people who chose to sacrifice comfort, safety, finances, families, and homes to bring equality to a country, and who then chose to forgive horrific acts of cruelty through the Truth and Reconciliation Commission. I knew I would never take my freedom or the peace in my life for granted.

Kathy presented our family with a coffee-table book, *Mandela: The Authorised Portrait*, which has the words of many transcendent South African leaders who endured unimaginable hardships while holding the truth and the freedom of Black South Africans as their goal. These leaders refused to compromise for less than one hundred percent moral justice.

As former UK Prime Minister, Gordon Brown said in *Mandela: The Authorized Biography*, "Of all the seminal events in the last 100 years . . . Mandela will be remembered as someone who showed us that people are essentially good."

> *"I always knew that someday I would once again*
> *feel the grass under my feet and walk*
> *in the sunshine a free man."*

> — Nelson Mandela, *Long Walk to Freedom*

Red Soil

A land of red soil covers my shoes.
It clings to my ankles and dusts my face, making
my brown skin ruddy and bronze.
This land coats my hands, my heart, my thoughts:
The thundering hooves of impalas on the plain,
The still, silent pose of the acacia umbrella thorn tree,
The chorus line of longhorn cows whose lean stomachs sway
side-to-side.

I smell the sky in Africa.
Remembering two smooth-rumped glowing giraffes nibbling
leaves in the lamplight of our van.
The early morning chill is still in my mouth with the spice of tall
grasses from the thatch roof and walls.

This mother continent holds me tightly in her womb loving me
as the child of hers that I am.
Why did it take so long to open my eyes in her dawn?
I am a newborn in awe of her ancient light.

Now awakened, my skin vibrates African:
Table Mountain high, Soweto deep, red
moonrise on Lake Jozini,
Songs of Zulu children in my ears.

Before my Ingwavuma friend, sitting beneath the Fever Tree,
gives her last breath to the AIDS demon,
I will send my soiled rands, a
prayer for her revival.

8

CROSSING THE ABYSS TO ME

When we returned from South Africa, Carlos spent most of his time in his studio, and I worked upstairs in my office or at the Santana office. I continued my New College classes and wrote an essay about our South Africa sojourn that I titled, *Literature as Inquiry: Through the Lens of South Africa*. I noted that the 1986 rally we had attended on Central Park's Great Lawn to oppose South Africa's system of apartheid was the beginning of my activism for the cause. Recalling those early moments of involvement in the struggle had highlighted the gravitas of our trip with ANSA.

I was uplifted by our meetings with activists in South Africa. The decades they had worked to eradicate apartheid gave me a fierce strength. I was still processing for weeks and months afterward, but the trip had accomplished what the Arch had hoped it would when he invited us: We were all inspired to live in solidarity with the South African people. They had achieved victory, although there was still work to be done. I returned to my daily routine with Mandela's smile shining in my memory.

Santana released a new CD with a single featuring singer Michelle Branch, then went on tour and performed on TV shows in support of the record. When the band returned, I held our annual office retreat. Carlos didn't attend these as they were workshops for staff, not the band. I sat at a U-shaped bank of tables in a hotel conference room with the road crew and office management team, listening to the challenges each person faced in their work. My goal with these workshops was to improve communication and share team-building practices to further the band's success.

A corporate consulting expert led us through a series of exercises to help us explore our temperaments, needs, and motivations in our work relationships. There had been a recent injury with a member of the crew that concerned me, and I wanted to be sure all avenues of safety and systems to prevent injuries were examined. As chief operations manager, I had always searched for information to support our staff.

"I had an idea that I read about in a management publication to do random drug testing on the road. It really worked in the company I read about and could foster a drug-free and safer environment on tour," I suggested. The article impressed me because employees in that company had taken the testing seriously, and it had improved their productivity and personal lives.

There was complete silence in the room. I looked around the table at the guitar tech, the drum tech, the road manager, and production manager, searching for signs of agreement.

"We'll never be able to implement that on the road," the tour manager said.

An assistant to Carlos declared, *"What happens on the road stays on the road,"* and laughter and smirks followed.

His comment alluded to secrets and activities only they were privy to. My body shook as I imagined staff knowing about my husband's sexual liaisons that I worked so hard to deny. My chest tightened, and I felt suffocated listening to the banter.

The facilitator seized control of the conversation, encouraging everyone to discuss why my idea might not work. *"Let's stay focused on what Deborah suggested. There was a lot of verbal and nonverbal response."* Her voice trailed off as my mind raced, and my heart tightened in frustration. In that moment I felt far from positive professional growth and maturity. It was as if the music industry was run by teenagers who still wanted to cut class and get high, thinking they were getting away with something. The road staff were laughing at my wish for Santana to tour with a drug-free environment while I viewed it as a tool to bring the best to our audiences.

After the session, the staff mingled in the bar, and I drove home from the hotel, knowing I was finished pretending about my life. I was a prisoner in a world of someone else's making and did not want to be part of an environment with high-risk behaviors and a lack of responsibility. I had built the office culture on a set of values to follow that included respect, safety, legal guidelines, and shared goals. I had never dreamed others would think it a joke.

I wanted to live in a fresh, peaceful atmosphere, not an immature world of selfish ambitions. I was also fearful of what Salvador might already have seen and experienced when he traveled with his dad on the road.

Santana's music filled so many lives with beauty and joy, and we regularly received letters and emails from fans describing their transformative experiences. I guessed I was the one who was out of touch. One part of me was numb; the other was filled with holes, with places that atrophied each time I found out Carlos had been with another woman. I was sorrowful that the man I fell in love with when I was twenty-two, with whom I had shared over three decades of marriage, created three beautiful, talented, gracious children, and with whom I envisioned growing old, did not love me—not in the way I deserved and wanted to be loved.

The weight of the wedding rings on my left hand became heavy. A wave to a friend caused me to notice their tarnish. Opening a book, my fingers strained under the weight. It was as if the gold band and two diamond rings on either side held the broken promises of my marriage—the burden of the love I had ached for but was unable to capture. I decided to take the rings off, to allow myself to be free. I was still married, and I was overly conscious of my finger's nakedness, but I left the rings off and offered no explanation. Carlos had taken his gold band off years earlier saying he couldn't play his guitar while wearing it.

No matter how many times I attempted to explain that my life was as important as his, his needs had taken precedence. In the early years, I believed that I could convince him to share my life, to turn his attention to me, for at least a portion of our time together. But his career had proved insatiable, and my efforts to share my life with him were unfulfilled.

I was from the generation of liberated women who said: *"Your ideas and lack of understanding of female power will no longer constrain us."* Yet I was not standing in my power. My wedding rings had given the world a false image of my marriage: I was not whole. The rings, if meant to symbolize an unbroken love, did not signify that for me.

I began to want a solo life, to live without the burden of suspicion about Carlos's infidelity and be open to new possibilities for myself, but I felt naked without my rings. On a walk, I passed a store in Tiburon and saw a luminous braided white platinum band in the window. I walked inside and tried the ring on. The diamonds sparkled and shimmered, drawing my eyes into the glimmering light. It was like meditation. I bought the new ring and wore it to announce my marriage to the light of my soul. I stored the old rings in a drawer. Carlos never asked me where my rings were. I suppose he never noticed the change.

Without telling anyone, I began searching for a new house to move to with Angelica. It would be my fresh start. Salvador and Stella were both in Los Angeles. I would visit them to tell them my plan but not until I secured a new residence. I tried to visualize what it would feel like to live with my own values and not function within a chaotic life I couldn't control. After thirty-four years, I had a difficult time imagining what life would be like without Carlos, but I had to cross the abyss to me.

———

I FOUND A HOUSE IN KENTFIELD with a view of Mount Diablo and a valley of trees. I worked with the accountant to purchase it, swearing him to secrecy, telling him I would speak with Carlos soon. I planned the day I would tell Carlos I was leaving, making sure Angelica was away from home.

When the day arrived, Carlos was in the living room on the couch holding his guitar in his hands, playing along with music on the stereo.

"Carlos, I need to talk with you."

He looked at me.

"*I need a separation.*" I didn't have the courage to tell him I wanted a divorce.

He pointed the remote at the stereo system and turned off the music.

"*I can't continue like this, and I need six months to figure out who I am. I don't believe you can be true to me and not sleep with other women. It's too painful for me. I have loved you for a long time. My parents loved you so much.*"

I was sobbing, my words tumbling from my lips like the staccato blurts of a trumpet.

"*I . . . have . . . to . . . see . . . if . . . I . . . can . . . find . . . love . . . for . . . myself.*"

"*Deb . . .*"

That's all he said.

He just stared at me.

"*I need six months by myself,*" I continued. "*I'm going to move out. I don't want us to communicate. I am too attached to you. I need this time, and I need you to honor my request.*"

Carlos's face was ghostly pale. "*Deb . . . No. You stay here. I'll move out.*"

"*I already have a place. I don't want to stay here. Please.*"

I knew I needed to cut off all communication and breathe into myself. I had to find out who I was without being Carlos's wife. There was nothing in life I wanted—no material goods, no vacations in Maui, no fabulous dinners in five-star restaurants, no trip to Paris or Kyoto. I wanted nothing more than freedom from deception and, even though separation was the most painful choice I ever made, I had to stop ignoring what I knew was true: Carlos would not change.

He slept in his studio that night. The next day he went out with his dear friend, Gary, and brought me back a gift. He was jovial and acting as he always did when I made a declaration of not wanting to continue with things as they were. But this time my spirit had flown; I was already gone—mentally, emotionally, and spiritually.

Sunday morning, he packed a suitcase and a guitar in the trunk of his Mercedes and drove to a hotel. I left for church, feeling that I was breaking our family, something that appeared to the outside world as whole.

There was no visible crack, no open wound, yet I felt the canyon in my body. I knew I had to be faithful to what was true for me.

I had always thought we would be married forever. It was what I wanted. I had been monumentally in love with Carlos, and I knew that some people never have the gift of that wondrous feeling, a soul connection.

There was a deep bond in my promise to love and cherish "until death us do part," and even though the Dalai Lama says, "*in disagreements with loved ones, deal only with the current situation. Don't bring up the past,*" I had to include the past now.

The hurts of my marriage had left cracks in my heart. And though I had forgiven and forgotten many of the incidents, my soul commanded me to move on. Was it that Carlos was complacent—so sure of his importance, value, achievements, that he thought I would never tire of his absences, his incessant working, his infidelities? I honestly thought he didn't need me or my love since he was fulfilled by his fans' adoration. I was surprised by his shattering, his sheet white face, cowed shoulders, downcast mouth. The Houdini of the guitar had no more magic with which to escape my needs. The finiteness of time on this plane of existence and the fairness of karma had risen. I felt no joy in his pain but couldn't rationalize that he had no inkling that my years of pleas were not empty threats. He had taught me how to be alone.

Always with profound change and cleansing, human nature grieves. In my anguish, I vowed to put my trust in God and stay on my journey. I felt as Emily Dickinson wrote, "*I am out with lanterns looking for myself.*"

9

RESPOND TO EVERYTHING IN LOVE

On March 10, 2007, I left Bay Way—after twenty-one years in the house that had held the powdery scent of Angelica newly born, of vanilla candles burning in the darkness during early morning meditation, and of fresh-baked chocolate chip cookies on fall afternoons when the kids returned home from school.

Packing up to move from that house of memories, my body felt like it was made of stone. It was arduous for me to take clothing from the closet, fold sweaters, pack dishes into boxes—dismantle my married life. Carlos's security guard, Chad, whom I had hired and who was a good friend, and my assistant Meshelle, his wife, helped me finish packing. They loaded the final breakable items into their car, one of which was me—carrying my toothbrush, a Fuji apple, and a tissue in my hands.

Stella flew up to help, but she and Angelica were immobilized by the trauma of moving from the only home they had known; Stella was eighteen months old when we moved in, Angelica moved in the day after she was born. Each of them was stunned, sitting at the kitchen table with downcast eyes, unable to finish bringing books and photos from their bedrooms. Salvador was in Los Angeles, lucky or unlucky to miss the final day of transition.

It is impossible for anyone to know what ending one phase and beginning another feels like without experiencing it firsthand. I didn't believe anyone around me knew the crevasse I lay in. I didn't think they saw how deep the holes were behind my eyes. I would never again misjudge the devastation of the end of anyone's relationship.

I released my life partner of thirty-four years so that I could survive. I allowed myself to grieve a prodigious loss, feeling that each footstep was leading me farther into the unknown.

My friend Ellen was a ballast in the storm. She was my chiropractor and holistic doctor, and we had become friends when Angelica and Ellen's daughter, Gabrielle, were in preschool. Her work was her life, her office crowded with patients interested in finding root causes of ailments, not masking symptoms with allopathic antibiotics and other medicines. We both began meditating in our twenties. Ellen knew the stress of my marriage had affected my health, and I confided in her first about leaving. She checked in on me every morning. *"How did you sleep? Do you need me to do anything?"*

I responded the same each time, *"I am good. One day at a time."*

I was confident I had tried everything in my power to have a healthy marriage and could not change anyone but myself. I accepted that the people I loved could traverse this life only with their own passions and beliefs guiding their choices. I had to start anew and allow the past to be the past. My grief would abate as this magnificent God journey continued to unfold.

I heard my sweet mother whispering, *"Respond to everything in love."* Spirit nudged me to be still as I rode the crest of the anxiety wave and finally settled down. I wrote, read, and attempted to calm the nervousness I felt after making this decision.

Our tour manager, Kevin's estranged wife, Lynn, had passed away the week before, and I dressed to attend the funeral. Kevin was our friend and had been the band's deal-making executive for more than twenty years; he took the band around the world with his impeccable supervision. I wanted to attend the service to support him and their children.

I drove to Novato, a small town north of San Rafael, and walked into the church. Kevin and his son, Ryan, greeted each person with a hug, their lips struggling to stay steady. His daughter, Nicole, sat crying in the front row, a teenager trying to understand how her mother could have died. Many of the Santana staff were seated in pews around the small Catholic church, but Carlos did not attend, having flown to Hawaii with a friend to nurse his wounds.

I scooted into a row wearing a wreath of sorrow for Lynn's death, which coincided with the death of my marriage.

Ryan stood tall, a high school basketball star who often stayed with the children and me when the band toured; I knew him so well and loved him deeply. He carried an air of fragile love for his mother when he introduced the priest to say the eulogy. At the end of the service, hugging the children, I almost burst into tears in their arms, but I would not allow the jagged edge of my sorrow to dim the jewel of theirs.

Driving back to my Kentfield home after the service, I took an exit on the freeway to Sir Francis Drake, rather than my usual Central San Rafael. Entering the gate to my new home, I saw that Meshelle and Chad's car was gone, and the dogs greeted me with wagging tails and wet kisses. I wandered through the rooms, becoming familiar with the layout of the house with its glossy wood floors and crown molding. I spent my first night in a new bed, in a new universe, the smells so different from Bay Way, the view over the valley sprinkled with lights of other homes where families were still together, a silence so still I dared not move and disturb it.

———

DURING THE NEXT WEEKS, I WAS DISTANCED FROM who I had been for over three decades. I had had no idea that almost all my relationships and connections with friends and acquaintances would be severed. I resigned from my position as vice president of Milagro, the nonprofit foundation I helped create, and resigned as COO, vice president, and co-owner of Santana, the business I managed for thirteen years. In the first month of my journey, I received a barrage of phone calls and pleas to return to my marriage, to not strike out on the path I had chosen.

Most of the people who called me had seen Carlos and felt sad for him, not knowing my story and the years of loneliness I had endured. Even friends who knew that my decision was not sudden but one I had mulled over and struggled with for many years, found it challenging to stand with me. The question I had to answer was: Did I believe I could live my life to its fullest, or would I settle for living what others thought was best for me and sacrifice self-esteem, respect, love, and kindness?

I was apprehensive navigating my new identity. Sometimes in the quiet of the night, I was startled by a sound in the garden. My smart, beautiful mother had lived with anxiety, and because she was emotionally strong and a fierce advocate for our family's well-being, it wasn't until I was an adult that I noticed her unease in certain situations. *"I need to sit on the aisle,"* she said when we entered a movie theater, one of Stella's volleyball games, or Salvador's music recital.

My worry about Mom had mirrored a tension in me as I was on high alert to protect her. But now this unease was mine as I became accustomed to a new home and a different schedule without my work at Santana. My meditation set a tone of peace, and each morning, I opened my eyes to sunlight, warm air, and birds cooing and twittering outside in the trees. God's peace was abundant. A part of me questioned how I deserved such freedom and beauty—such bliss, really. Mom's spirit hovered above my head, blessing me. God's heart beat in mine, and tears of gratitude slid gently down my face.

A transformation came when I was invited to attend Al-Anon. I didn't know much about it, although I had heard of Alcoholics Anonymous. It wasn't as though I considered Carlos's smoking marijuana or drinking a problem, and I drank wine and enjoyed the social camaraderie with friends myself. But Al-Anon was a revelation of my co-dependent behaviors. I had attempted to control many of Carlos's choices, thinking I could make him tour less, spend more time with the children and me, be faithful to me. In meetings, I heard stories that sounded familiar, illuminating that I had spent years reacting to Carlos's life, rather than leading my own. Al-Anon used the term "higher power" to describe a faith I must keep—a faith that the journey I had chosen would guide me to new perspectives and ways to be in relationships with my children and others.

Al-Anon meetings were held in various locations around the county. I attended a women's group, which felt safe. I couldn't compare my life to anyone else's, yet I resonated with a woman who said, *"I wanted to believe we had a wonderful home environment because that was true some of the time."*

Sunlight filtered through the large windows at the side of the room. The hazy rays made me blink, or was it the tears starting to fall? I, too, had touted our wonderful home environment even though I was often lonely, solo parenting, and trying to manage the volatility of Carlos's career and his choices to put his career above us.

I had compared our family structure to those of doctors, nurses, surgeons who worked hundreds of hours, to athletes, airline pilots, and journalists who traveled frequently and whose jobs took them away from home. I had excused what caused me pain because I had accepted the life I chose when I was twenty-two.

Buddha wrote:

> *"How will you become free? With a quiet mind*
> *Come into that empty house, your heart,*
> *And feel the joy of the way beyond the world."*

I added various modalities of therapy, including Emotional Freedom Technique (tapping) and counseling with a therapist who used Eye Movement Desensitization and Reprocessing. Many of my memories were blocked or hidden. My therapist asked, *"Do you try to protect others by concealing the dysfunction in your marriage?"* My heart beat like a mallet on a large drum. *"I guess I wanted the world to have the image they believed— that all was well in our home."*

I continued to dive into the ocean of my new life, and my fears took a back seat to calmness and confidence as I worked on freeing myself. I thought, *"This was why people hesitated to leave relationships that were unhealthy or even abusive."* It was vigorous, unrelenting work to change patterns and required a bravery I had to nurture every day. It was no small task.

With my new attorneys, I set up a donor-advised fund at the San Francisco Foundation and wanted to name it "Do a Little" in honor of Archbishop Tutu's words: *"Do your little bit of good wherever you are. It's those little bits put together that overwhelm our world."* My mission would be to serve women and girls in the areas of health, education, and happiness. I emailed the Arch and asked permission. His response: Yes!

I needed to move out of the Santana office and create a new life, but where would I work on Do a Little granting and Salvador's music business? I sometimes had public events that Meshelle managed for me as well. Ellen was there for me again, offering me office space above her holistic health clinic in Mill Valley. It was a large, quiet, and welcoming room, and a comfort to know she was just a stairway away.

I asked Meshelle if she would leave Santana. *"I know I hired you to manage the fan club, and now you are an administrative assistant, but will you consider coming to work with me? You will be my personal assistant."* It was a difficult choice, but after a day of reflection, she said, *"Yes,"* and accepted the new job, moving my computer, personal files, art, and awards from the Santana office to Mill Valley. Our one-room space was on the same level as the treetops, and the shaking leaves of the birch and bay trees were new music to listen to while we worked.

I BEGAN TO TRULY EXAMINE MY IDENTITY. Who was I in this new iteration? I no longer had a partner through whom my existence was filtered; no husband that I clung to. I no longer needed to hide, cover my face, close off all expression, or put on a "Mona Lisa smile" beside him. I had hidden myself for years, behind a self-imposed mask of composure, and I was happy to be free with the discovery of the new woman I was becoming.

Now, I picked up books that awakened new insights about who I was. I heard my goddess voice telling me to seek and give affection from the fountains of springs rising from Mother Earth's core. I searched for my underlying dreams. In his book, *Living the Wisdom of the Tao*, Dr. Wayne W. Dyer wrote that the Tao asks, *"What is my own nature if I have no outside forces telling me who or what I should be?"*

I felt like I had been in a chrysalis for the past few years, and now I was at a precipice of beginning to know myself outside of it—no longer bound by my past. This freedom urged me to be gentle with myself, to release my ideas of what a good, meaningful life consisted of for anyone other than me. It had been easy to identify myself by my marriage, summer trips to Europe, the abundance of rose bushes and apple trees in our garden, or by my three children, their beauty, and how well they did in school.

But what constitutes a glorious life is the liberation of hearts and minds.

I wanted to live in harmony with my inner nature and feel secure following my instincts and intuition. I wanted to speak confidently, tell my truth, and express my emotions without fearing judgment. I desired to attract people into my life who could honor, respect, and love me.

My life had slowed down to a state of coherence; my rushing about to accomplish tasks and meet with lawyers and staff were long gone. I called this year "my coma year" as I couldn't really feel yet—so much was in the process of being reborn.

I discovered that Mom had been right—about yoga, how easy it was to make biscuits, and me doing too much for other people and not knowing how to rest. While she was alive, I didn't comprehend the truths she saw for me. I felt I had to do something, everything, for everyone. I thought that was what God intended for my life. Help the woman on the corner with the sign: "Homeless. Need Food." Stay up past midnight to complete unfinished office work or to do laundry, exhausting my body in the process. I didn't understand how powerfully God moves when I am still. Nor did I see how intricately linked surrender and acceptance are.

I had nowhere I had to be, so every afternoon I sat in meditation or read books about healing the inner person. Working through the Al-Anon program, I applied compassion and understanding to Carlos's actions that had hurt me. My higher power could infuse me with strength and humility in all my affairs—with family and my interactions with others throughout the world—and I carried God's principles with me.

At times, I felt happy realizing that the love I needed was inside of me. I stopped drinking wine to mellow out my evenings and allowed myself to accept the ebb and flow of my varied emotions. I went to yoga classes to relax and calm my body. The layers of my understanding about myself began to roll back, revealing that I had places inside me that were not loved. These broken connections began long before my marriage—maybe as a child being dropped off at kindergarten and feeling alone on the playground or perhaps hearing about racist acts in my family history. None of my life experiences were tragic, but I still shoved my feelings down when they were too upsetting.

I began to look at inner love, knowing that I did not need to earn it or work for it. I only needed to be receptive to it and believe I was worthy of loving myself.

My stomach rolled with nervousness as I felt the edge of this truth—believing in and loving myself included me accepting myself and all my imperfect ways. One afternoon after another, like feathers floating in a sky of timelessness, grace held me up, as if something larger than me had me under its arms and was flying me along on an exhilarating ride.

Each day, I was at zero, completely empty, learning to live all over again. I was at the base of the mountain, beginning my climb to enlightenment. The chirping of birds awakened me, and each nightfall I left the day's struggles behind. I struck the match to illuminate my world, as though I was opening my eyes and seeing for the first time.

10

GRADUATION

Even as I was reveling in my newfound freedom, I continued to push myself in my quest for knowledge. My studies at New College placed me in an academic environment with people whose educations had been interrupted like mine and were dedicated to earning bachelor's degrees. The campus was in the heart of the Mission District's thriving, diverse culture with taquerias, vintage clothing shops, three-story Victorian apartment buildings, and stores with used books and records. I drove into San Francisco, found street parking on side streets by squeezing my car into small spaces between driveways, and climbed stone stairs to classrooms. The faculty was progressive, and the students were an eclectic group. The readings, discussions, and professor lectures were cathartic—and provided me with a lifeline to keep my nose above the waves of uncertainty in my new solo life.

In the interdisciplinary studies program, I attended classes two weekends a month, learning about political and global issues, as well as literature and the arts. I loved amalgamating all the information and writing papers expressing what I learned. I struggled in classroom discussions about critical thought, though. Everyone else seemed to understand the concepts of our thinking juxtaposed with world politics and economics.

I had been living in the world of spirituality, which was not open to debate, for the most part. So, it was grueling to be in my mind when I wanted relief through Spirit, but studying kept me sane, challenging me to absorb new philosophical frameworks and sharpen my analytical tools.

I studied late into the night, reading *The Emergence of Cultural Studies and the Crisis of the Humanities* by Stuart Hall, and attempting to digest the concepts of transnational feminism and the myriad oppressions of people in different societies. My mind was expanding in the crystallization of new thoughts.

Through the program, I made new friends: people whose lives and thoughts I admired. It was refreshing to meet people who knew little about the music industry and had different focuses in life. Like Natalie, with whom I walked to Lucca's Deli to buy salads and sandwiches on our lunch breaks. She told me, *"My babies are with my husband. I want to teach when I receive my degree."* She was also a poet with close ties to her homeland of Israel.

Returning to college was a kindness I gave myself. Academia was a world I had waited to visit for many years, and I flourished in it. Too many women die with unfulfilled lives, broken hearts, and unrealized dreams. Liberating my mind and spirit infused my life quest.

In my second semester, I began work on a novel using fractious border issues as my premise. When we lived in San Rafael, there was so much hatred towards immigrants who came from Mexico and Central America to work here. The vitriol toward these hardworking people was appalling. As Dolores Huerta says, *"We didn't cross the border. The border crossed us."* In my novel, I wanted to humanize characters and tell the stories of atrocities that occurred so that migrants had to flee their countries.

I'd learned about the work of scholar Marco Villalobos through oral histories he recorded and research he conducted in the African-rooted communities in Latin America. He was a 2003–2004 UNESCO-Aschberg bursary laureate, and his field of expertise was the historic towns of Mexico's southern Gulf coast, where traditions were inherited from Africa. He had a passionate interest in the small town of Yanga, named for a self-liberated slave, Gaspar Yanga, who was believed to be from a royal family from the African nation of Gabon. Yanga led his rebel band into the mountains and created a town of 500 freed slaves.

Through email with Marco, I asked him to meet with me to discuss taking a trip to these African-influenced towns. He came to the office, bending his head to get in the doorway. Tall and light-skinned, Marco had a wide smile. *"Hello, Deborah, thanks for inviting me."*

He gave me a copy of his book, *African by Legacy, Mexican by Birth*, co-written with Ayana V. Jackson, about the founding of San Lorenzo de Los Negros in Veracruz, Mexico, in 1608. Marco's work was exactly the history I wanted to explore.

"I'm excited to hear about the places you've visited," I said. *"I'm working on a novel about the third root—Afro-Mexicans who are considered the third major ethnicity alongside Indigenous and Spanish people. I'm hoping you might take me on a trip as my guide."*

"That sounds interesting," he said. Marco sat at the table and showed me a map of La Costa Chica and a list of Afro-Mexican communities. *"I've traveled to the Afro-Mexican communities of Oaxaca, Guerrero, and Veracruz, chronicling the existence of Afro-Mexicans. In the 1990s, the Mexican government acknowledged Africa as Mexico's 'Third Root.' For nearly 500 years, the existence and contributions of African descendants in Mexico had been overlooked, although they continued to contribute their cultural, musical, and culinary traditions to Mexican society."*

"Your expertise and fluency in Spanish will make this meaningful," I said. *"Please let me know if you can accompany me. I'll pay all costs."*

"Let me look at my schedule," Marco said. *"I'll get back to you."*

Marco emailed me that he was "in" and in the next few weeks, he mapped out the route we would take and what we would see. He decided we could accomplish what I wanted in a week. He scheduled interviews with Afro-Mestizos as a resource for my characters. I asked my New College advisor, Allyson Ritger, and my writing group friend, Jackie Luckett, to accompany us on the adventure that would begin with the origin of Mexican civilization: the Olmecs.

It was early May 2007, and I had been on my own for two months. I packed carefully and included a red cotton shawl that had become a talisman for me. It represented joy and power, and when I meditated, I kept it over my lap with both palms resting on my solar plexus. The pain of separation from my family receded when I breathed holding the cloth.

I was in the midst of working through the divorce and had selected a female attorney who understood I wanted fairness, a dissolution in six months, and little contact with my soon-to-be ex. Carlos was honoring my request to have no contact for six months so I could feel my own life. We'd spoken on the phone a couple of times and met in a park once. It was challenging, but I was adjusting to planning my own life.

———

ON THE AIRPLANE, AS WE FLEW ACROSS the California border to Mexico, my wedding rings were still packed away in a drawer and my new band was on my finger. Airplanes brought memories of the life I once enjoyed, battled, and finally left. For so many years, I flew through the skies with excitement to see unfamiliar places; I fondly remembered my visits to the Prado, the Louvre, Peruvian catacombs, and Kyoto temples.

Through the airplane window, the sky was opaque gray blue in its prequel to night. It was an in-between time of day, and I was in an in-between time of my life. Allyson sat beside me in seat 8B, reading *The Passion*, by Jeanette Winterson. She lifted her eyes from her book and said, "*My husband packed for me because he worried I wouldn't have enough outfits.*" Wow. I could never imagine a husband doing such a caring act. In the row in front of me, Marco slept off the previous week's cold. A few rows back, Jackie read an article about Junot Díaz in *Poets & Writers* magazine.

On headphones, I listened to Nina Simone with a women's choir— tambourines shaking, her hands on the piano, singing "My Sweet Lord," which triggered my memory of Salvador's School of the Arts' dancers bending in *pliés* and dancing the Pony across the stage to the same song.

For some time, I had wanted to let go of my attachment to all of the possessions I had in my life: too many silver and gold earrings, diamond pendants, fancy dresses; too many meals with the vegetables and meats trucked from faraway farms; too many candles (I needed only one to light the darkness); too many pens and cards; too many clothes and too many cars. There were only five people in our family, and we owned seven cars.

I had lost my way, my perspective, and the sweetness in my life, and I admitted that my marriage perpetuated a missed connection to my sacred self. I told myself that I had only now in which to expand and awaken my heart. Tomorrow would offer more information, deeper realization, and the unfolding story of my new life. What was real was that I had chosen myself: education, dialogue, sweetness, and self-love. It was all I wanted. No more excuses; no more angry words, isolation, distance, or people hiding behind substances to numb reality and prevent intimacy; no more blame or fear. I was risking all I knew to be free.

From the window, I saw a lightning bolt into a distant bundle of dark clouds, a flashing glimpse of nature's power. Then another strike sliced through the billowing formations as if illuminating the darkness I was in with a promise that I would be able to see more soon.

The airplane landed in Villahermosa, and I felt a strong inner call to release the past, accept the present, and see my heart mended. The past still clung to my ankles, but the future vibrated in my hands. A voice within spoke to me, and I wrote in my journal: *Catch your heart, Deborah, in the breath of God's dream for you. Look not at what has been but only at what is now. It is all you need. Mystery and magnificence are God's gifts at this moment. A perfection of all that you know will come; not a perfection in events or people but a perfection of purpose and a journey to peace that can only come if you continue with one foot in front of the other: for you, for your children, for the world.*

We stepped from the airplane into a night as hot as Dante's inferno, and my past seemed to incinerate into ashes that I imagined blowing away in the night air. Jackie and I laughed at the change in weather from San Francisco's fog. We took off our sweaters and found our suitcases. I rented a car, and Marco drove us past apartment buildings, a car wash, a Kentucky Fried Chicken, and an Applebee's on the way to our hotel, the Calinda Viva.

Villahermosa is a large industrial city; passing alleys, I smelled corn tortillas and heard children's voices and barking dogs. The next morning, we began with a lavish buffet breakfast in a simple dining room before we embarked on our drive to see the ancient Olmec sculptures.

Marco drove us to La Venta, a small city in the state of Tabasco, where a major excavation of gigantic stones was completed in the 1940s. We toured the museum site Olmeca-Zoque, located in the archaeological zone, with its exhibits of paintings and collection of colossal sculptural heads made of basalt and weighing as much as twelve tons.

These huge faces had flat foreheads, large noses, and full lips suggesting that Africans were in Mexico much earlier than the 1500s. Our guide led us through two exhibit halls with original stone heads and copies of others that had been moved here. It was remarkable to see these stone heads—some twice my height—with names such as Juchimán and Ixtlilton. The full-bodied sculptures were uncharacteristic of this area and historians thought that they were traded from other regions of Mexico.

Seeing their massive size and reading about the old ways raised the question of how the ancient people carved and moved these monolithic forms from one place to another. Did they roll them? How did they maneuver the twelve-ton artifacts onto canoes or rafts to float them to new locations?

I pondered these questions as Marco drove us back to Villahermosa, where we visited Parque Museo La Venta, the outdoor museum where many of La Venta's most famous basalt pieces now stood. A poet, Carlos Pellicer Cámara (1897–1977), fell in love with the Olmec culture and the pre-Hispanic heads. The government was planning to build a freeway through the sacred La Venta site, so he made it his life's work to preserve the ancient figures, and the park was built in his honor.

In a swamp-like lake, lights shone on three crocodiles eating fish. One of the crocodiles was eighty years old. We walked through a rainforest over two wooden swinging rope bridges and stood before a round, stone image, the moon hanging like a magnificent yellow-orange face through palm fronds.

The next day, we drove to Tlacotalpan, a colonial town that was a world heritage site and reflected the Spanish influence on Mexican culture. We walked on wide streets with one-story houses painted in bright corals, greens, pinks, and blues, and into the main zócalo in the center of town. We walked past a banyan tree whose trunk was white with bird excrement. Jackie moved to the middle of the street to avoid any bird droppings. Allyson said, "*It's good luck to be pooped on.*" We laughed.

We visited Iglesia San Miguel Arcáng with gorgeous turquoise and white tile floors and stations of the cross with statues of Jesus and Mary. I dipped my finger into a bowl of holy water and lightly touched my forehead, chest, and each shoulder, whispering, "*Please bless Salvador, Stella, and Angelica. Keep them safe.*" I placed one hundred pesos in the tin offering box. Jackie and Allyson took photos with their professional cameras. Jackie studied a glass-enclosed Jesus and two very faded red velvet rectangular pieces of fabric with a hundred tarnished milagros.

I welcomed the simplicity of this excursion. My life was stripped of its former glamour. I was not recognized as someone's wife or attached to anything, and not one person reacted to my last name, since Santana was a common Mexican name. Not only did I not receive the usual question, "*Are you related to Carlos?*" I often forgot about my former existence altogether, immersing myself in Mexico's historic land and studying ancient archaeological buildings and Olmec figures.

Each morning, I meditated as I did at home. I carried a leather travel frame with the children's photos inside and set it on the desk and lit a small votive candle. Breathing deeply, I closed my eyes and felt my breath moving from my solar plexus up through my chest and throat, exiting at the top of my head, my crown chakra. "*Bless this day,*" I prayed. "*May I receive your direction and align myself with your will.*" I recited the Unity Prayer for Protection for Salvador, Stella, and Angelica: *The light of God surrounds you, the love of God enfolds you, the power of God protects you, the presence of God watches over you. Wherever you are, God is.*

I prayed for protection for myself, too, and that I would have compassion for Carlos and for each human being's dignity to choose their own way. I prayed to speak kindly and not gossip but reason things out with experience, hope, and strength. There was still anger in me as I fought for my life. I opened the book *How Al-Anon Works* and read

Step One: *We admitted we were powerless over alcohol—that our lives had become unmanageable.*

Since my friend introduced me to this program of recovery, I practiced the tenets daily. Before, I lived a pattern of trying to control the uncontrollable: Carlos's schedule, his faithfulness to me, his desire, his behaviors. Al-Anon had many aphorisms that were encouragements for daily life. One I spoke almost daily was: *God, grant me the serenity to accept the things I cannot change, courage to change the things I can, and wisdom to know the difference.*

Being in the company of my writing friend, Jackie, my New College advisor, Allyson, and Marco's balanced male energy assuaged my heart. As we drove around, Marco gave Jackie the sobriquet "La Princessa," as she needed to sit in the front passenger seat to avoid motion sickness. We nicknamed Marco "Tope," which translated as bump, because as Marco flew down the roadways a hump would suddenly appear in the road, causing us all to fly to the ceiling of the car and bump our heads. We screamed "*¡Tope!*" and laughed wildly.

Marco had driven us from interior cities to the sea without ever complaining. He acted as professor and guide, an ideal man who was unbothered by our many requests to stop at restrooms and our need to be regularly watered and fed. He drove us through the countryside, and we stopped at Catemaco, a small town on a lake. Egrets were everywhere, perching on mango and oak trees.

Marco said, "*Let's go to the zócalo. I want to find a healer.*" Catemaco was known for its community of brujas and brujos. Marco drove to the center of town, and we parked near Parroquia San Juan Bautista. The white-tiled church had two towers and a tall iron fence where people stood behind tables selling candles, tacos, pastries, and carvings of Jesus and the Virgen de Guadalupe.

A woman was selling flowers, and Marco asked her name. "*Victoria,*" she said as he bought a small bunch of chrysanthemums and gave her ten pesos. He bent toward her and whispered in her ear. Victoria raised her right arm and pointed. Marco asked her, "*¿Puedes llevarnos allí?*" Victoria nodded yes, and we followed her. She stopped outside a house and Marco knocked on the door.

A man in a bright *azúl* shirt welcomed us inside. We said *"Adios y gracias"* to Victoria. Marco spoke with the man in Spanish, and we were ushered into a living room. *"This is Tito. He's a healer,"* Marco told us.

Tito said, *"Mucho gusto."* Marco told us the fee, and we all pulled pesos out. Tito guided us into the garage where there was a shelf with clear bottles of pink, green, and lavender liquids; flickering votive candles; and pieces of branches with their leaves intact.

Marco removed his white t-shirt and sat in a chair. Tito stood before him and began an incantation in Spanish, dipping a branch in the waters and spraying Marco with the liquid. Tito drank the green water, then spit it on Marco's chest. Jackie gasped, and I wanted to as well, but I remained silent. Allyson lifted her camera and took photos. Marco bowed his head to his hands after his cleansing, and I bowed in respect, but I couldn't keep my eyes off Tito's diamond pinky ring.

Marco rose and whispered, *"If you want a healing, please stay."* I shook my head no and followed him out of the room. Jackie and Allyson remained inside as Marco and I moved outside into the hot sun.

I waited a few moments and asked, *"What was that like? What did you feel?"*

Marco was wiping his face with his t-shirt, then pulled it on over his head. *"Crossing the threshold between his living room into his workspace, the air thickened. I could feel his practice like a blanket over me. The layers between the profane and the spiritual peeled back instantly."* He lifted his head to the sky and smiled: *"I could feel energy from the people who'd visited before us, their prayers, and the direct intention of Tito as a steward of messages and prayers. I was intensely aware of how confined I've become to the boundaries of my physical body, and after Tito's chanting of things that were airy and clean—clouds, unspun wool, fresh rain, spring water—there was a lifting of the weight that covered me when I entered. It dissolved, and with it, so did the boundary between my physical form and the Spirit world I was swimming in. Leaving the room, I felt lighter."*

I began to feel like I'd missed something by not having a healing, but my years of being with a guru had made me cautious about humans professing to have special gifts. I was happy being in the sunshine, waiting for Jackie and Allyson to emerge.

We were silent as Marco drove us to Xalapa (also known as Jalapa). The city was hilly, and we passed universities, museums, sporting arenas, and thousands of cars. The next morning, we toured the Museo de Antropología de Xalapa and stood before Head One, which weighed twenty tons. Its place in the dappled sunlight magnified the dark-gray granite sculpture with pock holes and African features. I felt the souls of the Afro-Mestízo people rising from the earth, and I understood the lineage and back-story to my novel.

The climax of our trip was in the eponymous small town of Yanga, where we visited the square dedicated to the escaped slave. In the sixteenth century, the slave trade brought almost 200,000 Africans to Mexico to work in silver mines, in homes, and on sugar plantations. In 1537, Gaspar Yanga was brought to Veracruz, Mexico, by ship and he escaped into the mountains with other enslaved shipmates.

Andres Maceda Martinez, librarian and a proud descendant of the Third Root, was our guide and took us to meet descendants of the enslaved African at Rancho La Lupita. Andres introduced us to the Peña Virgen family, who shared their ancestral lineage. I asked the matriarch, Zosema, *"Dónde fué su padre?"*

Zosema answered that her father was from Martinique. Slaves were introduced there in 1636, a century after Yanga and the African ancestors of this area arrived in Mexico. The Peña Virgen family members didn't openly exalt their African roots as Andres did and emanated a palpable protective air about their past as though resisting examination as representatives of the Afro-Mestízo culture.

Reserved at first, Zosema eventually warmed to us and took us inside her home, where we viewed photographs of her grandparents, who looked more Spanish than African in the faded photos. Jackie asked Zosema's daughter questions about her favorite foods, and I took notes while sitting beside the lush foliage—palm, hibiscus, maculí, and mango trees.

This family was like my own family of mixed blood, each person's skin a different hue. I explained in my halting Spanish the similarities of growing up in the US and being of Irish-English and African-American descent and feeling that people looked at our family members as oddities.

I wanted to connect, but I recognized that it would take more than one visit to get to know them and to hope that they might one day accept me. However, it was a beginning, an open door to a culture I had not previously known.

We were all tired from our long day as we headed for Veracruz—the port of entry for Yanga and thousands of enslaved people centuries ago—with the heat of the evening settling like dust on our skin. We passed stone walls and crossed bridges over brown rivers, my eyes following winding dirt roads to wooden homes. Small fires burned along the roadside with tendrils of smoke curling into the darkening sky. Mountains, where Yanga led escaped slaves to begin new lives in freedom, were visible in the distance. I imagined them racing through thickets of trees in the night, no longer shackled to plantation owners and slave traders.

We ate our last breakfast together, plates of chilaquiles covered in white cheese, fresh onions, and red sauce, accompanied by thick black coffee. I was sad our journey was ending. *"Marco, thank you for this trip. You have shown us a Mexico we could never have seen without you."*

He said, *"Thank you, Deborah. I am happy we saw the family at Rancho La Lupita and met your goals."*

We recounted our adventures, at ease in the morning sunlight, preparing to return to our lives. Once we arrived at San Francisco Airport, we hugged goodbye, the four of us going our separate ways after our odyssey.

Allyson had taken hundreds of photos, and I compiled scenes for my novel from her many images that captured the history and spirit of the Olmec civilization. But making up a story about borders and ancient Mexican cultures was challenging when all I could think about was my own story.

I was grateful for the hours and months of studying, which eased me out of my loneliness to concentrate on facts and add new ideas to increase my understanding of other cultures, but I set the novel aside to concentrate on completing my bachelor's degree in humanities. This achievement broadened my view of myself and reignited my intellect. There would always be more for me to learn, but I felt a sense of accomplishment earning my undergraduate degree.

THE DAY OF THE NEW COLLEGE CLOSING CEREMONY was a raucous celebration with students wearing boas over graduation robes and sequins sewn onto caps. Teachers called out, *"Please line up in alphabetical order. Last names beginning with N here. S's, please line up against the far wall."* I moved to my place, ready to follow the line of graduates into the Unitarian Church sanctuary.

When I heard the first notes of "Pomp and Circumstance," my bottom lip quivered; the song always gave me goosebumps, but this was my graduation from college after three decades, and I was shaky with emotion. All of us in the graduating class had faced challenges in working and managing families while completing our education, and I had made it through all of that while leaving my marriage. Kitsaun, Stella, and Angelica; Ellen, and cousins Emelda and Kimiko waved from a pew in the middle of the church. I wore an animated smile as I passed them with a sob caught in my throat that felt like barbwire. Students spoke eloquently about the thrill of completing courses, receiving degrees, and feeling successful. I listened, marveling that it seemed like a dream—ready to step out into the unknown with joy and adventure in my heart.

Over the span of a decade, I had taken courses at College of Marin, Mills College, and Dominican University of California, attempting to reach the academic status of Bachelor of Arts. Often, I felt as though I would never have the degree, yet in this moment, I achieved my goal during tremendous change and upheaval in my life. I celebrated, albeit from a detached mind and numb body, with everything occurring in a soft fog.

I hoped that completing my bachelor's degree would be an example of how I cared for myself and would act as an inspiration for my son and daughters. I transcended the mindset that had stifled and consumed me and vowed not to diminish myself ever again. In the fullness of recognition, I accepted that I and I alone represented my body, mind, and light. Such freedom!

I could now move my marriage into the museum of my history with gratitude for how my past had shaped me. The universal core of my truth was the declaration: *I am a spiritual seeker moving toward the light.*

11

WALKING
THE MOUNTAINS

I **PULLED** ON BLACK LEGGINGS, a soft yellow t-shirt with *Free Tibet* written across the front, laced up my neon Asics, and walked out my front door, up the steep hill onto Mt. Tamalpais. My ritual of morning hikes on mountain trails gave me silence to hear my thoughts without interruption, time to notice leaves that were green one week earlier were now a burnished gold, and to hear waterfalls crash down limb-strewn crevasses.

I was huffing just a bit when I reached the top of the incline at the intersection of Ridgewood, Evergreen, and Crown Road. I caught my breath and took a left turn onto the trail that overlooked the small town of Larkspur, with its church steeple that rises through an opening in the trees.

There were numerous protruding tree stumps and roots that I stepped over as I climbed higher on the mountain. Thoughts tumbled through my mind on this late summer morning: seating arrangements for my son Salvador's wedding celebration to his college girlfriend, Megan, and planning Stella's and Angelica's flights to Southern California for the event.

I passed a trio of women chatting and was grateful to be in my solitude, my footfalls the only sound I made. Heading down vertical wooden steps into the lush forest, a woman walked toward me with a golden retriever and an Australian shepherd dancing around her feet.

I nodded a friendly, *"Good morning."*

She stopped. *"Aren't you Carlos Santana's…"*

I interrupted her.

"Deborah. I am Deborah."

"Yes, of course. I've seen you on the path before. I was hoping I'd see you this morning."

She looked down for a moment before reconnecting with my eyes.

"My husband recently told me he wants a divorce. He's been having an affair, and he wants to leave me. I thought of you because I know you've been through something like this. I want to save my marriage, and my husband has agreed to go to counseling." Her voice shook, and her eyes filled with tears.

I understood her sharing intimate details with me even though we didn't know each other. She saw in me a kindred spirit. She believed I would understand the incessant thoughts she could not turn off, even on a hike on the mountain, the memories she clung to now that her marriage might be over. We were comrades in the desperation for options, in imagining how things could be. In the case of lost love, I shared her sadness. After all, I walked this same trail many times with my dogs after I left my marriage.

Like this stranger, I tried to save my marriage by going to counseling and talking for hours to try to understand and accept the impermanence of romantic love. Looking at her twisted face, I remembered the stabbing sensations in my heart knowing my husband had been unfaithful to our marriage vows, trying to compare my experience with the commonplace frequency of infidelity reported in the news, and wondering if we could go on.

I had been unable to persuade Carlos to change, and I had accepted that I needed to choose me, choose the truth in my heart. It had been three years since I felt those raw emotions of leaving married life. I had since committed myself to a steady process of healing and reworking my life and now lived in a safe, creative environment.

This woman's plight, her words of wanting her marriage to be whole when her husband did not, reminded me of the difficulty of brokering a deal with myself to be happily alone rather than allow another person's choices to diminish my self-worth. I wanted to be supportive of my new acquaintance.

"*You are on a journey,*" I said, "*the beginning of a journey to yourself.*"

Part of me wanted to warn her: Don't accept less than you deserve as a precious child of God. You will never be able to save this marriage because he has already declared he does not want to be with you by sharing his body and mind with the other woman.

I knew I couldn't tell her this—right then, she could only feel her fear and pain. She would have to delve into the elements of her marriage and her soul to know what would be right for her: to choose freedom or to accept the bumpy ride of trying to reconcile with her husband. From my own experience, I knew it would be a tender process. Reckoning came slowly. I tried to resurrect my marriage many times before I finally left.

She stood before me, not wanting to leave. I was waiting with her. "*I would love to take a hike together,*" she said. "*I'm sorry I blurted out my story.*"

"*Don't worry. I remember how hard it was.*" I had no pen to write my phone number so that we could continue to talk as she began the journey to herself, so I said, "*Go to my website and send a message. It will reach me.*"

We hugged goodbye and walked off in different directions, me in my unmarried life, filled with gratitude that I had peace and no worries about a husband being intimate with other women. I extricated myself from what I thought would be a lifelong relationship and divorced myself from an unequal marriage. This choice empowered me with self-respect and showed me that putting my faith in God and trusting in the ways Spirit moved in my life were invaluable.

Around another turn, Mount Diablo was visible across San Francisco Bay. I stopped and stretched my arms above my head, breathing in the scent of eucalyptus and acacia, the warm sun on my skin. Every cell in my body quivered with happiness as I recognized how far I had come.

I followed the path deeper into the canyon, the majesty of nature covering me in a canopy of oaks, bay trees, and madrones. A red-tailed hawk cried out overhead, song sparrows and kinglets chirped as they flew from one tree to another. I heard a creature scramble through the ferns and dry leaves and wondered if it was a bobcat as I walked alone with my imagination. The energy of sprites and spirits danced around me in the woods, and I noticed the knots in tree trunks and bird nests high in the branches. I felt the hard rocks jutting out from the trail and watched where I was stepping so I didn't trip.

Anton Chekov wrote: *"We shall find peace. We shall hear the angels. We shall see them sparkling with diamonds."* I believed this to be true, and ventured off into the unknown, trusting that I no longer needed to live for anyone else. I would find peace.

I was broken when I first claimed my life, but I was broken into pieces of me. All I had to do was put them back in a new order, into a beautiful puzzle of God's design.

I noticed I had not been paying attention to the trail. I rounded another bend and brought my concentration to the sunlight tracing the outlines of the madrones and casting shadows on the dirt. I began the descent to my house with a smile on my face.

I decided that I would tell my hiking friend that the journey gets easier, just as every hill we climb has a gentle slope leading us home.

12

THE GIRLS OF DARAJA

As my attunement with my spiritual source grew stronger, I welcomed new organizations to fund through Do a Little. There was a tremendous need for resources and empowerment in the Black, Indigenous, People of Color (BIPOC) community. For example, the median white household earned nearly 1.5 times more than the median household of color, and many communities with meaningful needs received lower levels of philanthropic funding.

Philanthropy was not new to me. Even when I was a child, my parents made sure we tithed and made charitable giving a part of our lives. Now, with my own charity, I could focus on women and girls to help balance the universe—to provide opportunity for the half of the population whose talents, intelligence, skills, kindness, and grace had often been overlooked or denied funding.

Although the nonprofit world spends most of its time raising funds for causes, I donated my own funds to Do a Little and learned to give a helping hand with little stress and immense joy. Approximately one-third of our grants fund women's rights and domestic violence organizations that provide a safe haven, health and human services, protective casework, and legal support for victims of abuse. These issues are important to me and often on my mind. I wanted justice for boys and men to break the cycle of violence but education to learn to prevent violence before it happens.

When I was younger, I worried that I would not see an end to suffering, wars, poverty, racism, abuse—the ills of the conditions of life. Later, I was still sure I would not see an end to these calamities, so my goal was to continue to set in place sustainable systems of change, equity, education, and interacting with the planet responsibly to avoid depleting natural resources and destroying ecosystems.

Through Do a Little's grant-making, I met people who lived with my same values and contributed to the world's betterment. One summer afternoon in 2009, a young teacher from San Rafael, Jason Doherty, came to talk with me about a free secondary school for girls he and his wife, Jenni, had started in Kenya. The two of them had recently cobbled the school together with the financial support and elbow grease of Jason's parents, Karen and Jack, the vision of Daraja's board of directors in Northern California, and family members and friends.

Jason met me in my office. Over six feet, three inches tall and broad shouldered, he embraced me in a bear hug. *"Jambo, Deborah."*

We sat at the round table, and I asked, *"How did you get the idea to start a school in Kenya?"*

"I fell in love with Africa when my parents took me there as a young boy. I'm a history teacher, and I taught at high schools in California, but my dream was always to return to Africa. I hoped to start a school there for girls. When I lived in Tanzania and Kenya, girls were the ones who were most often unable to complete their education. The Daraja Academy campus fell into our hands days before I was going to give up and postpone my dream."

Girls' education was one of Do a Little's missions. I already felt a connection with Jason's words, since I was looking for a group that I could bond with in the passion I held for educating girls, so I asked him to tell me more.

Jason leaned forward. *"These girls come from all over Kenya to our campus in Nanyuki. Some girls are still married off so that families can receive a dowry. Our girls would not be able to attend high school if Daraja were not open because their parents do not have the money for uniforms and books, which are required for every Kenyan student. Every girl has a different background—some are from the slums of Nairobi, some are from small villages in Eldoret or Marsabit, but what they all have in common is that each one was not attending school. Our first class on campus right now is twenty-six students, but at our peak, we hope to have 400 students."*

He opened his laptop and showed me a video of the school, with American volunteers cleaning windows and painting walls, the library with books lined up on shelves, and a few photos of teachers and students in the classrooms. Daraja means "bridge" in Swahili, and Jason said that Daraja Academy was a bridge for less-privileged girls to receive an education and move beyond poverty in their communities.

I was drawn to the girls' lucent smiles and bright eyes captured in photos on Jason's screen. He gave me letters from four girls, and I read their profiles. They were happy to receive an education, and one girl shared her "belief that education is the only key to success, and without education one can be useless." Another wrote that she "would like to be a doctor."

Jason and I soon said goodbye, and I knew I would support Daraja Academy. The girls' spirits had crossed thousands of miles and landed in my heart. They were symbols of my African family and a glorious community for me to intersect with, part of a culture I longed to know more about. I wanted to build a relationship with the students and staff to expand my circle of giving. To start, I offered to sponsor four girls' educations: one scholarship from me, and one from each of my children.

Jason later said with a laugh, *"This was a cold call . . . and those don't usually work!"*

Do a Little's mission to educate girls had no borders. For me, it didn't matter that Daraja's students were not in my hometown; what we did to uplift girls anywhere reverberated to girls everywhere.

Around the world, girls are often married at an early age to ease the financial burdens of their families. In many cases, parents must choose between sending their daughters to school or having their help in the home. Cultural traditions also impact girls' education more in rural areas than in cities. I read the girls' stories over and over; every one of them faced significant hardship, and each of them with a dream of bettering their lives. During the day, I remembered their faces, and at night I dreamed of traveling to Kenya. I emailed Jason and Jenni asking to visit the Nanyuki campus.

They suggested arriving at Daraja when the new Form Ones, the freshmen, would arrive on campus in February. The girls I sponsored would become Form Twos, or sophomores. I planned the trip with my assistant, Meshelle, accompanying me, and with husband-and-wife filmmakers Barbara Rick and Jim Anderson, who had traveled with our ANSA delegation to South Africa.

Barbara and I had produced and directed a short documentary film about ANSA's work with orphans, titled *Road to Ingwavuma,* and showed the film at festivals to raise awareness about the continuing HIV/AIDS pandemic. When I invited them to Kenya to create a documentary about Daraja Academy, the three of us would be producers, directors, and support crew. We would manage the schedule to shoot footage of classes, the campus, and my interviews with the girls.

As our plane descended in Nairobi in February 2010, I noticed the sky arced like a bowl of infinite blue as far as I could see. I looked out over the land where wheat-colored grasses and arrowroot trees stretched for miles. Flying over the outskirts of Nairobi, there were small farms, and in the distant city center, skyscrapers and tree-studded parks beneath the tips of our plane's wings. Daraja was three hours north of Nairobi, and Barbara and Jim had camera equipment, rechargeable batteries, light filters, microphones, and a few pounds of snacks—granola, nuts, and protein bars. As I walked outside baggage claim, a luscious, sticky heat settled onto my skin.

Jim drove our rented Land Cruiser out of Nairobi with the patience of Job. Each roundabout seemed to take us farther from our destination, Nanyuki, and kept us in Nairobi's pulsing, sweltering confusion of oil-spewing buses, crowded streets, and roads shared with goats and cows. Women walked through traffic with baskets of fruit and canisters of water on their heads.

Barbara looked at a map. *"I think this is the road, Jim."* Jim looked at her with furrowed brows and turned onto the roundabout. Meshelle had fallen asleep with her sweatshirt covering her face.

My eyes were wide, taking in every Kenyan nuance, though my head sometimes rolled about from jetlag. Men walked to work in hotel uniforms, some carrying bundles and baskets on their heads, and police blew whistles at wildly driven *matatus*—the brightly painted minivans that stopped along roads to pick up passengers. They drove with their side doors wide open, passengers and cargo bouncing along precariously. Even when the *matatus* swayed, bending almost horizontally, no one fell out.

We took a turn into high rolling hills of lush green tea plantations, the wet dirt a bronze-flecked vermillion. Soft, clear air blew through my window. Children walked on the roadside, boys in khaki pants, and girls in long skirts and ruffled blouses. When we reached the rolling hills of the tea plantations, I wondered if any Black Kenyans owned the land on which these tea corporations farmed.

Workers in red-checked sarongs, their heads covered with kerchiefs, carried woven baskets on their backs, tossing leaves over their shoulders and inside the baskets. Hectares and hectares of stunning beauty, from an African fairytale, or maybe the leftover plantation life where Africans were held in servitude to the Europeans—I couldn't tell.

Finally, the four of us were on the proper road to Nanyuki. The land grew arid; the hillsides and canyons reminded me of the road from Santa Fe to Taos. Each small town had a row of one-story buildings painted green, red, and white—housing chemists, pubs, and butcheries with hand-painted names over doorways with bespoke advertising. One was called the Obama White House Pub. Along the side of the dusty road, men and women perched behind boxes and bright plastic buckets piled with mangoes, potatoes, and green bananas for sale.

Nearing Nanyuki, the land expanded to plains, and acacia trees stood as monuments dotting the landscape. Masai men wearing red capes and beaded necklaces walked with camels, their tall figures striking and bright against the straw-colored land. Men carrying tall staffs led their cattle, hoping to find a stream or river with the brown running elixir to save their herd after a year of drought.

I embraced the peripatetic pace of the land—my mind slowing like the swaying of the thin cows—moving with the schoolchildren carrying books in their arms, not hurrying back home, not dawdling, but lingering in each footstep, their eyes catching sight of butterflies or following our lumbering Land Cruiser with our tired, foreign faces staring out at them.

Jason called Barbara and said, *"I'm worried you'll miss the last turn off. I'll meet you in Nanyuki."* We pulled into the small town and Jason stepped out of his battered and ancient-looking SUV, shouting, *"Jambo! Welcome!"* He gave us quick hugs and motioned for us to follow him.

We lurched past a large rock painted white with "Daraja Academy" written in blue, and rolled through the metal gate, where a furor of activity greeted us. Jenni bounded toward us, her turquoise-blue eyes reflecting the Daraja t-shirt she wore. *"I'm so relieved you've finally arrived!"* We climbed out of the car, Jenni embracing each of us. *"Welcome to Daraja,"* she said.

Dust-covered, tired, and cotton-mouthed, I allowed myself to be led to the dining room where the girls awaited us. Although I'd seen videos of the campus and classrooms, I was surprised by the bare walls and how wobbly the screen doors were. I already knew the school had no electricity, only a generator that worked in the evening. We scooted onto benches at long wooden tables, twenty-gallon aluminum pots on a table at the front of the room with cooked vegetables, *ugali* (a cornmeal mush), chicken stew, and urns with water. I was glad I had packed ten Fuji apples from California—a snack for each afternoon—as fruits and raw vegetables were a luxury the school couldn't afford.

Dinner was in full action in the concrete-floored hall with windows all around. Three campus dogs tried to sneak in the open door, while the brown faces of twenty-six girls looked up at us with piercing eyes and shy smiles as they sat on stools around the tables. Benedictor was across from me, Mercy beside her. Faith, one of the young girls I had seen in the first video Jason showed me in Marin when I became smitten, gave me a hug, followed by Christine, who was tall, with a wide smile, and said, *"Hello, Mum."*

Some of the students led us on a tour of the dormitories and class-rooms, teaching me "*jambo*" (hello), "*schule*" (school), and "*asante*" (thank you), my first Swahili words.

The girls told us about themselves and the small villages they came from. Faith said, "*I grew up in Naibur, just a half mile away. The only school close to us was five miles away.*" Fourth born in a family of six, Faith excelled at Daraja. Mary K hugged me, her nose crinkling as she smiled. She was seventeen years old and had not been able to attend secondary school because her family was unable to pay the necessary fees. But, she said, "*My mum pushes me to work hard, and I am the dining hall prefect.*"

Benedictor's black hair was cut close to her scalp. Her strong legs hinted she was a powerhouse on the soccer field. "*I'm from Kibera,*" she said. It was a slum in Nairobi with more than 250,000 residents, the largest in Africa. Mary P was as tall as me. She spoke softly, bowing her head. "*I grew up in a pastoralist family. We had to move whenever the cows needed greener pastures.*" She finished in the top three of her primary school graduating class even though she also had to help with chores and rear her younger siblings. I was proud and grateful to sponsor these remarkable young women.

To be chosen for scholarships, the girls endured rigorous interviews with Daraja heads of school and staff to ensure they did not have the financial means to attend secondary school. They were also asked, "*Why is education important to you?*" Every student accepted into the Academy showed an aptitude for becoming a leader, interest in the environment, and a desire to be a friend to her sisters, no matter what tribe they belonged to. This was key to Daraja's intention to do its part to heal tribal animosities from the political wars in 2008 that left hundreds of homes burned to the ground and more than 800 people killed.

We were finally escorted to our *rondovals*—the simple cement-floored huts with a wooden desk; closet; bed with an extremely hard, thin mattress; and a lone light bulb hanging from the ceiling. The bareness of my room evoked in me an openness to what I was about to learn in the school and from the girls. It made room for something new to be painted on my heart's canvas.

I awakened after my first night in Kenya, roosters crowing in a background of lilting birdsong, whistles, and chirps in soprano and tenor tones. At home in California, the birds in my garden sang in duets, but opening my door in Kenya, the layers of notes sounded like a symphony, an overture of nature's splendor.

Mt. Kenya rose in the distance behind campus, a sacred vision to the Kikuyu tribe, who believe the mountain is God's abode and built their homes facing it. It stands 17,057 feet above sea level, with its sharp, rocky peaks often shrouded in clouds.

Daraja's campus was enclosed by a fence: sixty acres protected from wandering giraffes, camels, elephants, and lions—just mongoose, cows, goats, chickens, and roosters ran free, along with a feisty bustard who spread his wings and hissed at me when I walked close to a certain bush that was obviously his habitat.

I began to learn the landscape: the rutted, dry roads of red clay; the sun rising each morning behind Daraja's campus, like a spotlight on the Turkana village; drifts of pink clouds against the soft blue sky. I was told that young Turkana men went through a rite of passage at the age of fourteen, which included pulling out one of their bottom teeth with pliers without showing any pain.

A few kilometers outside the gate, the tiny town of Naibor's tin shacks and distressed, leaning buildings reminded me of Khayelitsha township outside Cape Town. A few Daraja girls came from Naibor, a few from Nanyuki, others traveled hours from their tribal lands in Isiolo, Nairobi, Makindu, Dol-dol, Isibania, and Juakali. The roads to these locations were usually dirt, and in some villages, only a few girls ventured off to receive a secondary education. Daraja Academy's mission was to find girls who wanted to learn, even if it meant leaving their families to do so.

Walking from my rondoval across the soccer field to the library or Jenni's office, I felt how much I had changed and grown in these three years on my own. I was proud of the way I'd done the challenging work to spread my own wings, grateful to belong only to myself.

It was difficult to remember when my identity was still attached to my ex-husband's, and I was small beside his fame. It is an illusion that self-worth exists only in worldly success and acclaim. Inner satisfaction comes from so much more. Now I was free, part of humanity in radiant compassion and love. I felt that I was made of the same elements as the woman standing in line at the bank in Nanyuki, and the beautiful waiter at Mt. Kenya Safari Club who came from President Obama's Luo tribe. I saw my children in the neighbor kids who ran down the hill behind campus, chattering and laughing, so small with their books in their arms, so responsible at six in the morning, unaccompanied by adults as they traversed the countryside in bright, tattered clothes. I was in the embrace of all of humanity, no greater or smaller than any other person. At Daraja, my happiness confirmed that I was experiencing a rite of passage to myself.

———

THE GIRLS WERE IN CLASSES, WAITING FOR their "little sisters" to arrive in a few days. Barbara and Jim filmed the Women of Integrity, Strength, and Hope (WISH) class as Jenni taught the Four Pillars that held up the school:

1. Be accountable for the role that you play at Daraja, neither neglecting nor abusing it.

2. Maintain open communication. Speak honestly and listen respectfully.

3. Embrace differences. Treat all with dignity and respect.

4. Each day, leave it better than you found it.

"Memorizing and applying these pillars to their lives increases the girls' self-esteem and guides them to find their voices," Jenni told us.

I identified with all the pillars, especially wanting to leave each day better than I found it.

Jenni was in the front of the class. *"Open your dictionaries to integrity. What is the meaning?"* Pages turned as eyes peered at the definition. Hands shot up.

"The quality of being honest."

"A state of being whole and not divided."

"Incorruptibility."

The girls aspired to live these values in their family of varied souls: Muslim, Christian, Catholic, from city slums and country villages. They lived together in academic excellence, sharing chores, getting up early each morning to scrub floors and wash tables, staying up late to study alone or in groups, holding positions of governance within the dorm, playing sports together, and being effusive about their educational adventures.

The girls spoke about what they wanted for their futures. Tall and stoic, my sponsee, Mary P, folded her hands in her lap, *"For me, when I came here to Daraja, I wanted to be an engineer, but now I am sure I want to become a pilot."*

"I want to be a doctor," Winnie said.

Lillian smoothed her gray wool skirt and smiled. *"When I finish my secondary education, I want to help as many children as possible so they can get an education and be someone in life, just like me."*

I was moved as each of the girls, liltingly, expressed their dreams. They were poised and thoughtful, exuding dignity when speaking about their education.

Barbara found a perfect area where we could interview the girls, in front of colorful towels and clothing hanging to dry on a clothesline outside the dorm. We set chairs in front of a bougainvillea bush brimming with pink blossoms.

"Benedictor, please tell me your age and where you are from," said Barbara.

"I am sixteen, and from Kibera, outside Nairobi." Her voice was so soft I had to lean close to hear her.

"How do you feel you have changed since you came to Daraja?" asked Barbara.

Benedictor put her fist in front of her mouth and began to cry. I was stunned. I reached out and laid my hand on her arm, holding a space for her to tell her story of Daraja Academy. *"I am so happy to continue with my secondary education,"* she said. *"My mom came to pick me up to go back home for break because she missed me so much. She said she could not believe it was me because I had grown so big, and it seems Daraja is a never-never land."*

Being on campus, where the only electricity came from a generator that ran each day from 6 pm to 10 pm, I was discomfited by the excess of my material possessions. I loved my home in California and appreciated it as a beautiful abode of peace, but we in the developed world have gobbled up resources that could be shared with others. Since Angelica had left for college, for instance, I had lived alone in a four-bedroom house.

Walking from my rondoval to the kitchen, the mellow cows chewed on grass, glossy blue-winged starlings flitted from fence post to acacia tree, and the girls sang as they waited in line for breakfast. The air carried an ancient essence of civilization, or perhaps I was romanticizing this land I claimed as my own. Even the camels standing beside the road from Nanyuki stared as if they recognized me.

The opportunity to receive an education at Daraja Academy was something each girl had chosen and even prayed for. The annual tuition was $2,500 for room, board, uniform, socks, shoes, books, and sports. My film about the school would be a call to action for sponsors in America to pay a girl's annual tuition. Because girls were often not pushed to attend school, the importance of being able to finish their schooling greatly improved girls' lives. For each completed year of primary school education, girls' eventual wages increased by 10 percent to 25 percent. Girls who stayed in school for seven or more years typically married four years later and had two fewer children than girls who were forced to drop out.

Each time we ate together in the dining room for breakfast, lunch, or dinner, I was struck with how full I felt. The school had no refrigeration, and the stove was outside, built into the earth. There were no protein products unless the school chickens provided eggs. Jenni decided that when the chickens were slaughtered, they would add much-needed protein to meals. Chef Ruth began preparing meals with her small staff at six am. Breakfast consisted of porridge, bananas, sometimes sliced oranges, and always boiled water to drink. Meshelle and I were the first non-workers to tiptoe into the cook's domain seeking hot water to make my black tea and Meshelle's instant coffee. *"Good morning, Ruth,"* we said, feeling like we were cheating to be in the kitchen before anyone else. *"Habari za asubuhi,"* returned Ruth.

The sun shone on the wooden table where the cooks simultaneously prepared lunch while setting up for breakfast. My first sips of hot tea were like nectar, and we watched the girls step out of their rooms, carrying towels and wearing sleepy faces before they began chores.

On Sundays, the students gathered in three classrooms to have church services: Catholic, Christian, and Muslim girls worshiped in different languages, and sang praise songs. I sat on a wooden bench under a silver oak tree and listened to their clear, strong voices, not understanding what they were saying but feeling reverence and a knitting together of their hearts. Mary K came outside from her church service and sat next to me.

"What are they singing?" I asked.

"How the Holy Spirit will help them," she said with her combined King's English and Kenyan accent. Mary K's duty as the kitchen prefect was a responsibility that included making sure everyone was fed and that tables and benches were tidied after meals. Mary K had a gravitas, a deep composure and maturity that struck me as someone who had shouldered responsibility and accountability in her life.

Meshelle and I hiked around campus and saw small houses where the staff lived with their families, hung clean clothes on outside clotheslines, and enclosed goats behind crazily leaning tree branches. I heard the generator hum at six pm each evening, happy we would have electricity for a few hours, even though I fell asleep by nine, waking at four am to write and listen to the curious sounds of animals. One morning I saw the exquisite beauty of a full red moon hanging in the sky above the plain.

I remembered the Turkana and Masai mothers who had walked their daughters to their first day of school at Daraja, and the girls who wanted to be doctors and teachers and believed in the future of their dreams. I also believed.

There were many things that Daraja needed: water, solar power, laptop computers, textbooks, and a new dorm. But there were many things Daraja had that could not be bought: respect for humanity, and the students' excitement to learn, the teachers' dedication to expand the girls' horizons, and the girls' promise to live bright futures and change our world.

On our last night together, we gathered in the cafeteria for the girls' talent show. They sang traditional songs as well as the official Daraja Academy song, their pure voices reserved but strong. Eyes shone in the battery-operated lights. Jim brought his guitar and sang a folk tune, strumming the strings as the girls howled with delight. Benedictor and Christine handed me notes: *"I'm so happy to hear that you are my sponsor. . . . I'm feeling so sad that you are leaving. I will miss you so BIG. I love you, Christine."*

Benedictor wrote: *"I will miss you so much because you are near me. You are like my mom . . . I want to wish you a very nice journey back home and as you go to continue to do your work, remember Daraja as one of your favorite things to do . . . May God keep you for long and add you more years to live in your work . . . I love you BIG."*

I paused outside my rondoval, letting the infinite stars and the girls' words hang in the black sky.

We rose early to drive back to Nairobi. The sun had not yet risen; chickens were just waking up and scratching in the dirt. My heart was heavy leaving the friends I had made and the girls I loved. As we loaded our suitcases into the Land Cruiser, Faith, Christine, Benedictor, and Mary came to say goodbye. They had already finished their chores and studied by flashlight. They cried in my arms. I cried, too.

We drove into the sunrise, glowing at Mount Kenya's feet.

———

Inspired by the stories of the Daraja students and committed to raising funds for their scholarships, I sought partnerships in San Francisco and across the Bay Area. With help from the San Rafael Daraja Education Fund office, I became an ambassador for the school, showing the *Girls of Daraja* documentary and holding fundraisers in Sausalito, San Francisco, Los Angeles, San Diego, and New York. Other collaborations included the San Francisco Arts Commission, which agreed to host a joint art and social intersection project with San Francisco high school girls and the Daraja fourth-year students: Daraja Means Bridge Cultural Exchange.

World Savvy, a leader in global education, developed a ten-week arts education program that used technology as well as visual and literary arts to encourage an international, cross-cultural exchange. The program would bridge the cultural gap between eleven high school-age female students in San Francisco and fifteen students in Kenya.

Each group completed their writing exercises with teachers in their own land, then we brought the girls together via Skype to talk to each other. Everyone made a special effort to facilitate the exchange at 8 pm for the San Francisco group and 6 am for the Kenyan students. The Daraja girls' faces shone brightly meeting the American girls of color. Instructors left each room so the girls could share their life experiences and speak with autonomy. They later revealed they had honest conversations about circumcision, drugs, and how to navigate romantic interests.

One of the San Francisco leaders suggested we pay the girls a stipend for their participation. At first, I balked. The Daraja girls would not be paid, so why should the American girls? The Daraja students had their needs taken care of, including room and board, tutors, and counseling. The San Francisco girls did not have the same support and had responsibilities beyond school. The stipend would help with extra costs, as well as show them we valued their time and talents. This was an important lesson that I incorporated in my philanthropic work: provide fair wages for learning experiences that enhance students' lives. This knowledge inspired me to later support summer Leadership for Change internships at the Smithsonian Institution, which provided housing and a stipend for high school and college students who applied for and were accepted in the program.

Over the years, I received many letters from the girls in Kenya marking their progress, and I watched the school grow in the number of students. Graduates returned and were hired as trained counselors or launched themselves into the world becoming nurses, teachers, engineers, researchers, and NGO workers. They became advocates in their communities speaking out against female genital mutilation and early marriage and teaching dental health and hygiene.

I returned to Daraja in 2012 with my friend Vee. Each morning, we met outside our rondovals and walked past the Daraja rock and turned right toward Dol-dol Road. The mornings were quiet, our feet striding on sandy trails. Daraja's dogs, Ajax and Rasta, accompanied us. Vee laughed: *"I've never seen two happier dogs."*

At breakfast, we ate pancakes and drank chai, sitting with Alice, Shamsia, and Faith. Vee's profession as a social worker gave her an important insight into what the counselor at Daraja was experiencing, and they had a meeting sharing professional insights.

I took a photo with all the girls on the patio outside the kitchen. I was in the middle, my smile in celebration of the 104 students then in residence on campus. I later emailed the photo to the Arch, telling him, *"I spent ten days on campus with them, and I cannot tell you how brilliant they are, how eager to learn, how filled with love for God and community! They are my heart."*

He emailed back: *"They are gorgeous (and so are you!). Thank you for your generosity to them. You send out waves of love and compassion in a world desperately hungry for these. Love, Arch."*

My children also got involved. Salvador supported Daraja Academy through his music, gifting songs for two documentary soundtracks and performing at three fundraisers. Stella held a fundraiser in New York City, inviting her friends and the public, speaking lovingly of the school. Angelica created artwork for a booklet: *The Secrets to a Healthy Smile*, written by doctors at the NYU Department of Dentistry, showing the girls how to maintain healthy teeth and gums.

I am sensitive to the use of "poverty porn" to raise funds in philanthropy. This is the practice by content creators and organizations of distributing videos and print messages that highlight disadvantages and promoted colonialist exploitation. It is my honor to work with organizations that honorably serve those in need, and I raise the issue if I notice it. Respect and humble cooperation are my principles.

I love that I have been able to walk on African lands. Feet to soil; ancestors' spirits to my heart. Kenya gilded my body and mind. Every granule of red earth settled on me as wisdom. The haze of Nanyuki's streets with cars, bicycles, donkey-led carts, street boys with grime-encrusted hands held out, side streets with pounded-tin fences, and camels staring at me stayed in my mind. Daraja's ochre buildings with green roofs and classrooms with blackboards covered in chalk-written lessons, girls' voices calling out answers to teachers' questions; it is all a part of me.

One year, one student wrote, *"I am breaking for my holiday this week. I will send greetings to my family on behalf of you. I hope you will do the same to your family on my behalf."*

I remembered President Mandela asking our ANSA delegates to give his regards to the Americans. My sweet Daraja daughter asked me to carry her greetings to my family. And I did.

Since 2009, Daraja Academy had admitted 390 girls who have performed more than 7,200 hours of community service each year; 261 girls have graduated; 95 percent were attending or had attended college; and a new campus just completed construction to be an academic hub of social change. Big dreams and reachable goals because of the leadership and Kenyan teachers and staff. I haven't visited in many years, but the students and teachers have remained with me. I continue to support Daraja's intention to educate girls because supporting girls improves not only individual lives but also creates leaders and changemakers.

13

TRUTH IS EVERYWHERE

By March 2011, all my children had moved away from Marin. I traveled between New York City, where Stella lived, Seattle, where Angelica attended college, and Los Angeles where Salvador lived. Not only did I miss them, but I wanted to stay connected to their lives. I flew to visit, we met for meals and took walks, and they filled me in about their latest interests. I enjoyed being with them as adults, still being mom, but not in the former hovering way—more as one who listened to every word and saw how strong, loving, and bright they were.

On one visit to Seattle, Angelica drove me to Kerry Park on Queen Anne Hill; we sat on a bench overlooking the skyline and Puget Sound. It was a bright day, and the snow-capped peak of Mt. Rainier had come out from hiding.

Angelica and two of her classmates were creating a project for their sociology class on public space in cities. *"How is your film going?"* I asked.

"We were filming all over Seattle and had an appointment to interview a seventh-generation Indigenous man, John T. Williams. We wanted to ask him about public space for Indigenous people. We were around the corner from his woodcarving studio when he was murdered by the police for carrying a piece

of cedar and a small carving knife, a necessary tool for his trade." Her voice cracked with sadness and anger.

"What? Why?" I asked her.

"The police department is racist. We asked them for an interview, and they refused. But serendipitously, we found John's brother and interviewed him."

"What did he say?" I asked.

Angelica paused. *"He said there was no such thing as public or private land in his culture."*

She was learning hard, valuable lessons from First Nations people. Oppression and abuse were realities they coped with daily. Later, a John T. Williams Memorial Pole was erected to honor Williams and raise awareness of the traditions, history, and culture of Seattle's Native populations. The pole was carved by his family and friends and included depictions of a perched eagle, Mother Raven, and a figure of a woodcarver.

Back home, I continued turning the pages of my life, looking for inspiration and new ideas. I wanted to learn more and acquire a master's degree. However, I didn't want a degree that only stimulated my mind; I wanted one with enquiries into spiritual topics. I was still choosing me, choosing peace, choosing kindness, and choosing truth, which kept me on a quest for love and happiness in my life.

I returned to the book I had read when Mom was in the hospital and found wisdom in Sharon Salzberg's words: *The truth is everywhere, in all of our experiences. We do not have to fitfully try to have a sublime, magical experience and, in this effort, disdain what is actually happening. We do not have to struggle to find the truth. Every single moment is expressive of the truth of our lives when we know how to look.*

I discovered a local college, California Institute of Integral Studies (CIIS), which was the only academic institution that offered a master's and PhD in women's spirituality, where my interests lay.

I applied and was accepted into the program and attended an informational meeting for new students. I felt at ease in the five-story building in the heart of downtown, on Mission Street, a few blocks from MoAD. I knew I would be challenged in this academic environment. CIIS had been building the curricula and courses since 1968 and had rigorous expectations for students. In their words, CIIS "ventured beyond the boundaries of traditional academia through coursework and research that combined Eastern and Western spiritual and intellectual traditions."

I visited campus and purchased books for my courses. In the quiet of the Laurence S. Rockefeller Library, I spread my books across the shiny wood tabletop and breathed in gratitude.

———

My Master of Arts program in Philosophy and Religion with a concentration in women's spirituality began with the 2011–2012 fall semester.

One of my courses, "The Literature of Embeddedness," was an opening to eco-crit lit as a way of study and living. Ecofeminist alternatives to a dualistic interpretation of the world led me further away from patriarchal influences. I dove into the reading materials, which highlighted stories and activism of women traditionally omitted from the pages of history and established me in a world of womanist philosophical, scientific, and cultural paradigms.

When we stepped through the threshold of the classroom, my co-learners and I were asked to leave behind whatever our day had been filled with. Some professors burned sage, walking in front of each student and waving the musky smoke to cleanse us. Arisika Razak, professor of womanist feminist worldviews, played music and asked us to stand in a circle. She said, "*We honor the Indigenous lands this building is on. We thank the Indigenous people who blessed the waters, the rocks, the trees, the animals.*" She began to sway and then glided around the room. We followed her moon-round, sparkling brown face, her braids dangling behind her tall, lithe body. I tried to move in her image, smoothly arching my waist and lifting my arms like a meandering snake.

For more than thirty years, Arisika had conducted workshops for women around issues of self-esteem, women's bodies, liberation struggles, and meditation. She told us, "*I really love the work I do that interfaces with the field of transformation, empowerment, liberation, and cultural reclamation.*"

As a nurse midwife, I really feel that reclaiming the sense of honor, reverence, and power for women's bodies is essential." In her class, I began to claim reverence for my body—three children born, wear and tear on my knees from running on asphalt, not blooming in a sacred sexual way. I absorbed Arisika's years of teaching the spiritualities of women of color and women of the African diaspora like a thirsty plant.

In "The Black Madonna and Other Women Divinities" class, I met Beth, who was studying for her PhD. She intentionally wore the same red shoes every day, explaining, *"I purchased these shoes in a thrift store for five dollars. I am going to wear one pair of shoes at a time until they fall off my feet. I am walking away from worldly things to know my path on this road to deepening in women's spirituality."*

She added, *"I'm a white girl from Kansas trying to walk a mile in someone else's moccasins,"* which surprised me but also made me chuckle because of how emphatic she was.

"You are hardcore honest and brave," I said as we walked to the local tea house. Beth had left her husband, an African prince, because she didn't want to live an exalted life or in the confines of the traditions and rules he expected of her. Unlike my mother, who had married a Black American man, Beth had married a Nigerian from a very different culture. Mom fit into the King family belief system and thrived; Beth left her husband to stay alive and be authentic to her womanhood.

Our professor, Lucia Chiavola Birnbaum, PhD, was a doyen of Black Madonna knowledge, leading students to Sardinia, an island where the African Mother Goddess was revered. She told us, *"I was an upwardly mobile little girl in an Italian-American enclave in Kansas City, Missouri. In the neighborhood, the women yelled at each other and looked after all the kids, but I was inside reading."* She explained that earning her PhD in the history of social sciences intersected with the African-American struggle and the free-speech movement.

It was fascinating to me that both Beth and Lucia were from Kansas and loved Blackness. I was in love with the entire Women's Spirituality department. I was especially enamored of the depth of the professors' knowledge and the etchings of freedom on their hearts.

Lucia told us, *"I see the Black Madonna as a metaphor for caring and sharing and healing and vision now. Earlier I saw her as compassion and resistance. There are dark women divinities all over the world, the earliest right up to the present, and they're rising."* She said that Spain had the greatest number of Black Madonnas in the world, and pilgrims traveled to pray before them. *"Our human species began in a cosmology of a harmonious universe, a world view in which we were one with the caring mother of everyone."*

My upbringing in the Christian world had not exposed me to matriarchal societies or Indigenous views that the world was a place of natural plenty and the earth a living Mother. My colleagues in the business world and the nonprofit sector didn't know that matriarchal social structures provided balanced guidance or that "the woman is in rhythm with the entire universe." The positivity and hope for our planet conveyed in the readings bolstered my personal philosophy that the God of my understanding was universally present in every person, every spiritual belief system, and everywhere at all times. Mine was not the God of religions but of hearts.

A search for alternative sources of spiritual knowledge could sometimes create great upheaval for the seeker. I had my own reckoning, admitting that religious institutions would probably never welcome all souls, but if we created a circle of interconnected believers, we could welcome everyone to the table. Some cultures can hear the earth talking to us, asking us to evolve in a "radical interdependence." It is the holy way.

In Namaste Hall, Joanna Macy brought a weekend workshop of "Active Hope" to a group of students from different disciplines. An ecophilosopher and scholar of Buddhism, Dr. Macy has taught "Work That Reconnects" around the world for six decades. She walked onto the stage, gingerly sat down, and said, *"Let us begin in gratitude. My being here is for the sake of life on earth."* Then she took a deep breath and smiled, her eyes resting on each of us, not hurrying to begin the teaching but inviting us into her heart.

She told us about a different kind of power from that of governments and corporations that generate conflict and only allow a few people to prosper. A more sustaining and inclusive way asked us to have "power-with."

Joanna used the example of Nelson Mandela, who collaborated with the apartheid government through discussion and a commitment to step toward peace so that South Africa could move from a "win-lose model of conflict to one aiming for a win-win outcome." I closed my eyes and remembered being in Johannesburg at Mandela's feet.

"Please form groups of two and face your partner," she instructed. *"We are going to role-play."* We were asked to imagine twenty generations forward, assuming humans would still be here, and ask each other what we did to save the planet from destruction and what gave us the energy to do so. I was in the seat of the present generation.

"I want to apologize to you that we didn't do better," I said to my class-mate, who was holding the place of twenty generations ahead. *"I want to apologize that I was too comfortable in my affluence, and I gave up marching against corporations and nuclear power and war, all the destructive machinations of our first-world privileged society."*

My lips began to tremble, and tears filled my eyes. *"I am sorry that I wasn't angrier and that I believed, for a while, that climate change was not inevitable, that I sat numbly in my beautiful house on the mountain."*

Now my classmate, twenty generations in the future, was crying too. I recalled what gave me energy to be an activist. *"We stopped eating grapes in the 1970s to support farm workers led by César Chávez and Dolores Huerta. We protested Coca-Cola and international banks that fed the apartheid machine in South Africa."* My classmate listened; our eyes locked as I spoke.

When the role-playing ended, Joanna said, *"The big picture of change emerges out of the many dots of separate actions and choices. What we can gain changes to what we can give."*

At the end of class, I was exhausted but energized—exhausted by holding space for the sorrow and destruction in the world and energized by being in a circle with others who wanted to help dismantle patterns of thinking that divided us. Joanna Macy's teachings were an offering of love to humankind, a guidebook to becoming active participants in the future we hoped for.

My final independent study project was to produce a documentary about the Women's Spirituality program with the thesis question: "What happens when women put their own experience at the center of their spirituality?" Merging my passions of writing, documentary filmmaking, and spirituality, I set about interviewing professors and students with filmmaker Robin Fryday.

One professor said of the program, "*We really want to rebalance the world and bring the sacred feminine forward.*"

A student commented, "*Justice is our movement every day toward harmony and balance.*"

The college added a clip of the completed documentary to their website, and my work was acknowledged in a lasting way. In May 2012, I graduated with my master's in philosophy and religion with a concentration in women's spirituality—hard, unique, liberating work that I carry within me every day.

14

RUMI AWAKENING

I BEGAN TO BELIEVE THAT A BROKEN HEART can open one to the Divine. I had long enjoyed reading Rumi, the 13th-century Turkish/Persian mystic and scholar, but in 2007, when I opened to myself, his words became an integral part of my life. The cracking open of my heart allowed Rumi's love for the Divine to become a translation of wonder in my consciousness.

I witnessed the lure of his words when I attended an evening of "The Poetry of Gratefulness" in Marin. A teacher and translator of Rumi, Coleman Barks, read, and audience members moved their bodies as if drunk and chanted "aah," as an affirmation of knowing or the kind of relief one exhales after a cool drink of water when standing beneath a burning sun.

I heard Rumi's words, but they didn't penetrate my shell. Then, at a yoga retreat, when I was most vulnerable and at the edge of remembering my true essence, one of the teachers read, *"Let the beauty we love be what we do. There are hundreds of ways to kneel and kiss the ground."*

I truly awakened to Rumi with those words, a flame of tears falling down my face and an extraordinary vitality shimmering within me. Not long after, I discovered Coleman Barks' *The Essential Rumi* sitting on my bookshelf—a gift from someone a decade earlier that I had never opened. I began reading and found "A Great Wagon," from which the yoga teacher had read those two lines, and I saw that the lines that followed were even more meaningful to me:

Out beyond ideas of wrongdoing and rightdoing, there is a field. I'll meet you there. When the soul lies down in that grass, the world is too full to talk about. Ideas, language, even the phrase each other doesn't make any sense.

Rumi's musings, his creative gift of connecting Spirit with body, became part of my morning ritual. Sometimes his words made me quiver, unable to catch my breath, because my nerve endings couldn't bear the emotions that arose.

During my Rumi awakening, two dear friends introduced me to a man, and I had my first date in decades. It had been four years since my divorce, and I was like a teenager—giddy when talking with this man on the telephone or sitting across a table sharing a meal. I began sending snippets of Rumi's poetry to him, careful not to copy the most impassioned lines, afraid he would think I was in love with him.

Sharing Rumi's brilliance created such an intimacy with myself that I couldn't resist trying to draw this man into the mystical poems. He responded in awe and understanding, even telling a friend of his, "*This Rumi is so amazing. Have you read him?*"

Every nerve ending in my body became alert when I read Rumi, and I wondered if the light of his quatrains would open my friend's heart in the same delirious way. Through Rumi, I hinted at loving but still hesitated to say those words. Wasn't it too soon? And was I feeling fondness rather than love?

The truth was, I wanted to be in an effervescent, eye-locking romance. The flower of my inner being was ready to open in veneration to all this man was. For six months, I flew to spend weekends with him, and we traveled to tropical destinations together. But this was only my first attempt at dating, and I expected forever.

After a tumultuous breakdown in communication, as we talked softly, trying to regain the place in our hearts where we had left off, I spontaneously said, *"Love you,"* in my tearful goodbye. He responded, *"I love you, and I miss you,"* completely surprising me.

His poetry continued. *"We are like a chemistry set."* He didn't explain, but I understood. His energy and matter—his past, his now, his being—interacted with mine and created an energetic response. Sometimes it was calm and loving, other times explosive and destructive. Our interactions were making electrical charges in our atoms. We were bound together by powerful forces. His definition of our ups and downs as a chemistry set put me at ease and turned up the corners of my lips.

As Barks wrote in *The Essential Rumi*, "Beautiful poetry can keep one on the verge of the oceanic annihilation in God. Rumi says we've been walking in the surf holding our robes up, when we should be diving naked under, and deeper under."

Reading Rumi was like rubbing fresh spices between my palms. I inhaled the savory leaves of tenderness, sprinkling them around the garden of my heart. Ultimately, the man and I—the friend introduced through friends—ended our intimate relationship. We were not the lasting connection I sought. But my love affair with Jalal-ud-Din Rumi continued as I wandered through his 3,500 odes, 2,000 quatrains, six books called the *Mathnawi*, and numerous discourses and letters. Those I understood made me cry with smooth, silvery joy.

15

UNSUNG HEROES OF COMPASSION

I HAVE MEDITATED EVERY MORNING AT 6 AM for more than forty-five years. Through every loss—my father's and mother's last breaths, the end of my marriage, the worries about my three children—I prayed for peace to the infinite Spirit of God that resides inside my being.

Before my father died, I sat next to him while he lay in his bed in an altered state of half dreaming, half awake, calling out to his deceased brother and sister in joyous exaltation. I witnessed him interacting with spirits on the other side of this earthly plane.

My belief in Spirit gave me confidence to be myself in the world, to trust that wherever I stood was holy ground. Yet here I was in the ballroom of the San Francisco Ritz-Carlton on February 23, 2014, leaning nervously against the wall—one of forty-nine people from eighteen countries—waiting to stand before His Holiness, the 14th Dalai Lama. It was holy ground because those of us in this room belonged to organizations that worked for the liberation of lives around the world.

I had resisted this moment of honor since Dick Grace, founder of Grace Family Vineyards and Grace Family Foundation, told me two years earlier that he was nominating me to be an Unsung Hero of Compassion. He and his wife, Ann, had birthed this idea of bringing together "compassionate individuals from all corners of the world—those who have dedicated the course of their lives toward helping others." He had asked His Holiness to join him in the endeavor, and the Dalai Lama had agreed.

A glittering, round crystal chandelier hung over the center of the room, and 700 guests, including Stella and Angelica, were seated at tables draped in formal white linens.

I was seventh from the end of the line—in alphabetical order. His Holiness sat in a golden armchair in the center of the stage, his magenta robes wrapped around his body, a matching magenta visor shielding his eyes. His hands were clasped on his lap, right thumb over left, fingers intertwined like a garland. A thick green velvet curtain draped behind him, from the ceiling to the floor, with three brocade thangkas sewn with images of Buddhist gods and goddesses encircled in red auras.

At the morning's breakfast with the leaders of the Unsung Heroes of Compassion—Dick and Ann, along with Elizabeth Share and Christine Wright, the guides and organizers of the event—we were told what to expect when we were presented to His Holiness, as well as how to react to the world leader. "*Focus on and enjoy every moment,*" Elizabeth said. "*The luncheon and ceremony will be over before you know it. Please do not touch His Holiness; you can imagine how long the ceremony will take, so keep the line moving.*"

It had never been my intention to garner praise for the work I did through Do a Little. My goal was to serve the needs of women and girls in the areas of health, education, and happiness without focusing on myself. However, Dick had told me when I resisted the honor, "*No one feels worthy, and no one has ever said 'no' to me.*" And here I was.

It was said that the last words of the Buddha were: "Make of yourself a lamp." My grandmother had taught me this also, but through the words of Christ: "Be a lamp unto the world." It had been part of my framework since I was a child, spending summers on her farm. Being a light meant filling oneself with good thoughts and spiritual treatises, living with love for all, and helping others have a better life whenever possible.

The Christianity I had grown up with was a traditional interpretation of the Bible. My faith was not blind; it was fortified by prayer and worship in my family church. What I had studied of Buddhist teachings showed that students were encouraged to search the sutras for verity and scientific proof that peace came because of practicing meditation and being compassionate human beings. I have been interested in spiritual teachings from different traditions since I studied the book *The Religions of Man* by Huston Smith in my undergrad at Dominican University.

Now those of us chosen to be Unsung Heroes of Compassion were chatting, getting to know about each other's work. Dick's laughter rang out as he walked through our ranks. He introduced me to an honoree from South Africa, Grace Mashaba. We had each received a red paper-bound program of the event with each awardee's bio, and I had read Grace's and a few others earlier. She had been an orphan who had suffered repugnant injustices by a white farmer who raped and abused her. She did not have a mother or father to protect or comfort her. I could not see scars from the brutal torture inflicted on her but knew that the farmer had taken her to the hospital to have her sterilized. She lived to give freedom to others and had founded three facilities to feed, tutor, and care for hundreds of South African children.

Grace wasn't feeling well that morning and held her shawl tightly around her arms. Thin and quiet and dressed in a red and turquoise skirt and blouse, she was slight of build. *"May I get you water or tea?"* I asked.

"Yes, please," she bowed her head toward me. I took her empty paper cup and filled it with water, returning to sit beside her. I held her weathered brown hand in mine, wanting to absorb and heal her wounds.

I saw sweet, bright Conor Grennan across the room and waved. Months earlier, at Dick and Ann's home in St. Helena, he had spoken about his work reconnecting trafficked children in Nepal with their families. The next night I had begun reading his book *Little Princes: One Man's Promise to Bring Home the Lost Children of Nepal,* in awe of his crazy zeal to walk miles and miles over treacherous mountains to recover children who had been stolen from their homes, imprisoned, and forced to work long hours in slave-like conditions. Conor introduced me to his radiant wife, Liz, co-conspirator in rescuing children.

I was seated at a table with Luc Janssens, a Belgian who had grown up and earned his PhD in California. He bent over his plate, eating fruit and eggs. I asked, *"Where do you work?"*

In his French-inflected voice, he told me, *"In Laos, with my Lao Rehabilitation Foundation."* He cared for disabled children; built schools, dispensaries, and hospitals; shipped tons of medical equipment and supplies; built clean water systems in remote villages; organized plastic surgery missions; and delivered health care with volunteer medical staff in rural areas.

Each Unsung Hero was unique, many working with pennies to change the lives of those who needed an infusion of hope and a way to be safe in the world. Each one's work mitigated people's suffering, and there was a common mission to serve with love and caring, often sacrificing personal comfort and well-being.

My spirit expanded in recognition and respect for the work these people did around the world. I had never stood up to Iraqi police or saved Burmese refugees from oppression while staring down the barrel of a rifle. Yet Dick's smiling face and love for me invited me to banish any feelings of unworthiness and take part in the blessing.

THE LINE WAS MOVING CLOSER TO THE STAGE, and I shuffled my feet closer as names were called. My new friends climbed the stairs to receive white, silky *katas* around their necks and red strings for their wrists, like a tying on of love.

Then there was the incandescent moment for me to stand in His Holiness's presence. I tried to feel my heart and stop the buzzing of my mind, but it was difficult.

I wondered what to expect when I would be face-to-face with him. When I reached the bottom of the stairs, Elizabeth caught my wrist and asked me to wait. *"They need to speak the name of someone not present,"* she said.

I looked up at His Holiness. Apparently, no one had told him the person wasn't present, and he beckoned me forward with his hand, peering at me from beneath his neoprene visor, as if wondering why I was holding up the flow of blessings.

I gaped at him, losing my peace, and worried what he thought about me not doing what he said.

Finally, my name was called, and I ascended the stairs, bowing to receive the white kata around my neck from a teacher and the red thread in my hands from a nun. In a flash, I was standing before the incarnation of holiness. He took both of my hands in his, clasping tightly. His brown eyes glimmered behind large glasses, and his cheeks filled out in a beneficent smile. I was transfixed and held my breath. And then His Holiness released my hands, and I walked to Ann and Dick, hugging them both and continuing down the stairs.

We all lined up on the far wall of the ballroom, waiting until each had received the hallowing. By then, we were one family, united in our breathless moments with His Holiness. The audience rose to its feet, applauding us, and my cells burst into thunderous recognition. One, two, three minutes passed, and there was still clapping. It was like lightning on my skin.

When the applause stopped, I tried to walk gracefully back to my table, but I was shaken, out of my body, melting into a new substance of life. Angelica and Stella hugged me, smiling, and kissed my cheeks. *"Congratulations, Mom! We're so proud of you!"*

I sat in my chair, but I was not there. I thought my soul had lifted above the ballroom through the chandelier's socket. I was in a wholeness beyond myself. I was overwhelmed by the potential of my being enhanced, changing me from Deborah before the Dalai Lama into Deborah, who had been touched by the enchanting purity and compassion of His Holiness. This wasn't because of the fame of the Dalai Lama but because I had felt a connecting energy of Spirit.

The red string vibrated on my wrist, and the kata draped like angel wings over my shoulders. Many lessons and awakenings spun in my mind: Do not judge, only love; be peace and compassion; remain open; forgive again and again.

Over the next few weeks, I read His Holiness's books and listened to his podcasts. What a wonder that we had technology to bring us closer to spiritual awakening. But it was the memory of his eyes on me as I stood at the bottom of the stairs that propelled me to peel away what no longer served me and to recognize I was connected to every person.

His Holiness wrote in his book, *How to Practice: The Way to a Meaningful Life*: "*Although we may be meeting for the first time, I accept everyone as a friend. In truth, we already know one another, profoundly, as human beings who share the same basic goals. We all seek happiness and do not want suffering.*"

This was my mantra as I engaged with life. Everyone wants to be happy, and no one wants to suffer. I thought of this as I worked with women and children who were hurting from a lack of food and education and from the governments that often tortured them. I thought of this as I read news of war and the abduction of children and violence against women. I saw His Holiness looking at me and knew I could make a difference.

I sent an email to the Arch thanking him for allowing me to use his words for Do a Little and receiving the Unsung Heroes of Compassion blessing. I wrote: "*Because of your love, I was able to receive the honor.*"

The Arch emailed back, "*I am so touched and so pleased that my holy friend had the good sense to recognize the immense good in you . . . Much love and Lenten blessings, Father.*"

Who needs anything else?

16

DANCING ON
THE WAY

Ten years after I joined MoAD's board of directors, another MoAD board member recommended that I be invited to become a trustee on the National Board for the Smithsonian Institution. The board oversees twenty-one museums, the National Zoo, fourteen research centers, and is based in Washington, DC.

National Board President Sako Fisher invited me to her home to onboard me. She and her husband, Bill, are longtime philanthropists and founders of the Sakana Foundation. I walked past brick pillars, sculptured wintergreen boxwood hedges, and a weeping fig to enter the gate of their home in San Francisco. Once inside, Sako ushered me into the front salon of the elegant and stately manse, saying, *"Welcome. I'm so happy you are joining the board."*

She was refreshingly open about the financial and meeting requirements and instructed me to bring sports shoes for the meeting in DC. if I wanted to join her and others in walking to scheduled meetings. Her black hair was cropped close to her face, and her slim figure and petite height disguised her bold, boisterous power.

Sako later invited me to a Smithsonian dinner for the Asian Art Museum in her home, with china and glassware fit for a presidential event.

She was full of joy, open, free-spirited, and a champion of the museums and other cultural institutions, raising millions of dollars in campaigns to advance the Smithsonian.

The Smithsonian Institution's purpose is "the increase and diffusion of knowledge." After joining the board, we trustees enjoyed behind-the-scenes private tours of the National Museum of American History, the National Portrait Gallery, the Renwick Gallery, the American Art Museum, and the zoo. We had events in The Castle, the original edifice completed in 1855, which is now the visitor center and home to staff offices.

In October 2013, LaTanya Richardson Jackson and I met in Washington, DC, to host an event at the Smithsonian Museum of African Art to screen the latest Daraja Academy documentary, *School of My Dreams*, which LaTanya narrated. My service on the National Board of the Smithsonian gave me unique opportunities to include the Kenyan school in programs, to show my documentaries, and to invite others to become involved with the school. Dr. Johnetta B. Cole, director of this museum, and LaTanya had been close friends for years; both were Spelman College alumni. Dr. Cole had been president of Spelman for ten years when they both raised significant funds in support of the historically Black college.

The three of us met for lunch in Dr. Cole's elegant office, surrounded by abstract and conventional works of art on the walls, hardbound art and history books on shelves, and photographs of Dr. Cole with President Obama and other notable figures. We engaged in conversation about the Smithsonian National Museum of African American History and Culture's building, which was currently under construction, and the work of Daraja Academy. I felt honored and energized in the presence of these two brilliant women.

LaTanya and I taxied back to the Mandarin Oriental Hotel, and she asked if I was dating anyone. I showed her a photo of the man I was seeing, and she dismissed the person I showed her. *"I have the man for you,"* she said, her beautiful dark eyes under arching brows staring directly at me. *"I've known him for years. He may not be ready, but I will call him. His name is Carl Lumbly."*

I was curious but didn't give it much thought as I was still in a relationship. More than a year later, when the man and I broke up, my friends Barry Williams and Lalita Tademy were sponsoring a play at the American Conservatory Theater, called *Let There Be Love*. Carl Lumbly was one of the main characters. I had a dream that LaTanya, Sam Jackson, and I were in Woodlands Market near my house on Evergreen and they introduced me to Carl. I emailed LaTanya and told her about my dream. She responded, *"I am on it,"* meaning she would call Carl and make plans to take me to the play.

As it turned out, LaTanya couldn't fly up for the performance, and I took my writing friend Jackie who had traveled to Mexico with me. Our seats were in the right orchestra, so close I felt like a spy. Carl didn't know about me yet, and I knew just enough about him to feel nervous, as if he could see me seeing him. The play was excellent, and Carl's role was Alfred, a retired police officer who lived in an isolated world and listened to Nat King Cole, whom he considered to be his musical friend. I observed Carl as a seasoned stage actor, and from the angle of my seat, I stared at his dark face and eyes.

The next day I wrote a card to him that had a Rumi quote on the front. I sent it in care of the ACT address on Geary Street and flew to DC for a Smithsonian National Board meeting. I included my cell phone number and told him about LaTanya's proposed introduction. A few days later, while I was boarding a bus for dinner at the Smithsonian Castle, my cell buzzed with an incoming text message. *"Greetings, Deborah, just received your lovely card today. Did LaTanya mention my fondness for Rumi, or was that simply coincidence? I love the play so much. It is a gift and a privilege to be part of it. I'm sorry I didn't know you were in attendance that night. I would love to meet you and see who is attached to such precise penmanship! Perhaps we could have tea and greet each other in the next week or so . . . Do you know Samovar? Looking forward, Carl."*

I was excited and a bit flushed, but I texted back, *"Yes,"* and offered two dates for our convening. I was nervous to meet him, but LaTanya called me and said, *"Carl is nervous, too. You are both good. It is time."*

On April 30, 2015, Carl and I met at Samovar Tea Lounge in Yerba Buena Gardens in San Francisco's South of Market area. I arrived first and waited outside the restaurant. I saw him before he noticed me and was immediately struck by his bent posture. He had stood up straight onstage at ACT, and something about him now emitted sadness. When he looked up and saw me, or who he thought I might be, he grinned. We introduced ourselves and sat shoulder to shoulder at a table looking out at other diners and city sparrows who flew inside the restaurant looking for crumbs.

Carl talked about his wife, Vonetta, who had died of breast cancer in 2010, showing me that she was still utmost in his thoughts; his son, Brandon; and his single existence now in an apartment near Lake Merritt in Oakland. I shared about my children and my writing, and I mentioned I had divorced in 2007 but revealed no names. Carl had no idea who I'd been married to.

Before we knew it, two hours had flown by while we consumed a mezze sample platter of hummus, baba ghanoush, and falafel, and drank multiple pots of tea. There were bursts of elemental sparks between us, but I was wary because he spoke so much about Vonetta.

We parted, and as I picked up my car from the valet, he walked to the theater on Geary Street to prepare for the night's performance of *Let There Be Love*. Later, he texted me, inviting me to walk across the Golden Gate Bridge before he left town. He was preparing to play a role that was shooting in New Orleans, and, of course, this coming and going for artistic performance was familiar to me. I brought him a card with flowery words and two tea bags for jet lag.

I loved that Carl seemed to enjoy hiking and exercise as much as I did. He wore a t-shirt, and his sculpted biceps, shoulders, and chest engulfed me when we embraced. In all my years growing up in San Francisco and living in Marin, I had never walked across the bridge. The 220 feet above churning waters felt much more dangerous from the sidewalk than from the roadway I drove across so often.

In his Shakespearean voice, Carl said, *"I've been meditating for nearly a year and currently carry around one of The Great Courses on* Introduction to Mindfulness Meditation.*"*

"I've been meditating since I was 21," I said. *"Not mindfulness, but a type of Bhakti meditation of the heart."*

The sun was shining, which didn't often happen on the Golden Gate Bridge during summer months, and I felt radiant in the orb of Carl's attention.

At our cars, I opened my door to get in, and Carl pulled me to him and planted a kiss on my lips that sent seeds of life sprouting through my body, sending signals that I was indeed alive.

We texted when he was away, and he shared that he loved being in motion and that he read more fiction than nonfiction. I texted that I read Dr. David Hawkins's books as well as fiction and nonfiction. When he returned from his travels, I invited him to take a hike with me in the hills above my home. We walked up Evergreen onto Ridgecrest Road and onto the King Mountain Loop Trail. He followed me on the narrow, winding path, beneath bay and oak trees, then I followed him, watching his long stride, broad back, and swinging arms. I jogged a few times to keep up, the fragrant greenery and wildflowers blooming on the hills an aphrodisiac. Every so often, Carl lifted his face skyward and breathed a deep inhale.

On the descent back to the house, Carl said, "*When I saw you at Samovar, I wondered who you were behind your sunglasses. You were so poised . . . canting forward slightly . . . inclined toward me.*"

I laughed at the thought I was poised when I felt nervous.

He continued, "*I remember the distance between us. Or, more accurately, the space between us in which I felt our spirits resting up against one another.*"

I said, "*I remember noticing the men at another table staring at us when we sat down, and me looking back at them for too long a time. I was thinking—I am so out of practice being in public with someone who is recognized. I have no idea how long I looked back at them, and told myself, 'Ay caramba— get it together, girl!'*"

We looked at each other and laughed, always in step, in the nascent union of us. There was a membrane of miracle dust, love, and hope surrounding me.

On my deck, sunshine beaming, our bodies shared electricity when our hands touched, but I did not venture into that space. He was wearing his gold wedding ring on a chain around his neck. It was a barrier for me. I wanted to ask him why he protected himself with a message of faithfulness to Vonetta and wondered if he knew how strong a moat-enclosed castle that ring was. I sat on the chair with my legs on the fire pit and my body stretched out toward him on the couch, and I could feel our physical connection. Carl took a selfie of us, our faces shimmering in the sunlight. When he showed it to me, his countenance looked lighter than the first day we met.

He took in each detail in a nuanced way, aware of everything surrounding him. He told me, *"It's how I memorize."* We walked back inside, and he watched as I opened the box of long, purple-tipped wooden matches on the opalescent tray next to my altar and lit three candles that sweetly scented the room. I assumed he was memorizing.

Before we said goodbye, we hugged and tenderly kissed, his arms wrapped tightly around me. Later, I emailed him about the wedding ring around his neck that caused me to feel like I was asking him to betray Vonetta.

He called, and his voice was deep and melodic when he responded: *"I am shaken awake by your words. I'm removing the necklace. Can I come over so we can talk?"*

It was ten o'clock at night, but I said yes. Later, I thought how this was like a movie, dramatic and exciting. When he arrived, he immediately wrapped me in his arms, loving, tender, and present. There was no wedding ring around his neck. To me, it was a revelation of what love could be.

The next morning, we woke up, and I stretched my body toward him, reliving our intimacy, the touching of my skin on his. We looked intently into each other's eyes and rested in our warm embrace. In the kitchen, I poured cups of English Breakfast tea, and we sat at my kitchen table, sunlight shining through the windows. *"Would you like to try writing together? I've studied writing with Natalie Goldberg. Have you read her books?"*

"No," Carl said.

"She teaches a technique of writing for ten minutes or longer without lifting your pen or editing. I usually do this daily."

Carl rubbed his palms together, as if conjuring a spell. *"Yes."*

I grabbed my journal from my office and a yellow legal pad for Carl. Teacups full, pens and paper at the ready, our topics were "running, last ditch, and women." Just as I had done hundreds of times, my pen scratched for ten minutes. We read our pieces aloud—closeness dizzying our hearts. I'd only written like this with other students of Natalie's. Sharing this liberating method of spinning words onto a page with Carl enveloped us in a celestial membrane.

It was as if the past had blown away like fragments of fallen leaves in the wind. Every day I was in Carl's orbit, waiting to commune with him through phone calls or texts, and writing new pages in our togetherness. He was in the final days of *Let There Be Love* and had discovered his role as Alfred was realigning his memories of his father, whose parenting had often been harsh. One morning I awakened from a deep sleep and sat at my altar to meditate. After saying prayers for my children, I distinctly heard Spirit say: *"I have delivered to you your soul mate. You will be called upon to be strong, patient, and compassionate as he carries a deep wound that has tentacles throughout his body."*

I sat and thought about what this could mean. I felt like Carl was my soul mate, but was it my responsibility to help him heal? Over the next few months, the words faded from my memory as I continued to know Carl better.

17

ALL THE WOMEN
IN MY FAMILY SING

MY WORK CONTINUED WITH THE SMITHSONIAN. Wayne Clough was the Secretary when I began my tenure on the National Board, and he invited me to speak at the opening of the Smithsonian Folklife Festival in June 2014. The annual international exhibition began in the summer of 1967. Its intent was to present programs featuring cultural traditions and was held in the atrium of the Kogod Courtyard in the American Art Museum.

This year China and Kenya would showcase music, dance, traditional foods, and cultural studies. I immediately thought of an Afro-fusion musical artist, Iddi Achieng, whom I had met in Nairobi two years earlier. I asked the Folklife Festival team if they would fly my Kenyan friend to the US to sing and share her messages at the festival through her rhythmic cultural music. The team invited her with other Kenyan musicians to perform. I couldn't wait to hear Iddi's voice again, her music full of feminist lyrics and uplifting energy.

I spoke on the stage at the start of the festival: *"Here we see our common humanity. It gives us insight into the way other people live. The Folklife Festival shows us there's an amazing world out there. It's a celebration of us all and our interconnectedness.*" I welcomed the artists, musicians, and scholars from Kenya and China. *"Please welcome to the stage my Kenyan friend, Iddi Achieng, and the other divas!"* I saw faces of new friends and others attentive to my words. It was an honor to launch the festival.

Carl and I had been together two months, and our lives were becoming entwined in the magic of new love. I was on a journey in a new land, moving carefully over the terrain and feeling happy. I invited him to my master's degree graduation dinner and introduced him to my children, to Kitsaun and Gregory, and to my goddaughter, Aisha, and her two children. We were traveling at the speed of light since Carl had taken off his wedding ring. Sitting beside me, I touched his arm. *"I'm so glad you came,"* I said. His dark eyes shone in the soft light of the restaurant.

"I couldn't be happier to celebrate you," he said. He turned to Salvador and struck up a conversation. I was at ease with his words. It seemed destined. We didn't have to work hard or push or pull. Our love partnership flowed with grace, excitement, and wonder.

Carl and I met for hikes and tea, and I invited him to attend church with me. He began rehearsals for a play, *Emperor Jones.* We continued our free-write sessions when we were together. This allowed us to know each other better, by reading our prose out loud, from topics like bird chatter, anguish, and luggage. Carl traveled to Berlin for a film, and I went on a writing retreat with friends.

Most mornings after meditation, I wrote in my journal, recording whatever rose from my being. Sometimes I lamented about the world, other times I wrote about my children—concerns and joys. I also wrote about Carl and where we were in our relationship letting my hand move my pen to express whatever was surfacing. Every cell of my being vibrated with a peace from God, a joy of the Divine, and a celebration of freedom. I was at home in a dynamic awareness that God was the Source, and each breath opened me to a life of wholeness. I continued to forge my identity and sought ways to express who I was meant to be.

———

IN JUNE 2015, MY FRIEND CHRISTINE BRONSTEIN came to me with a business project she was thinking about. Chris and I lived a mile apart in Kent Woodlands, and I met her through her community of female friends she named A Band of Women. Like me, Chris believed that if people stopped focusing on differences and started finding points of connection, we could change the world. She became one of my best friends, my ride or die.

Her three children were younger than mine, still at home, and she had the daily duties I had before—shuttling them to school, ensuring homework was finished, making meals, and shopping—all tasks I had stressed about when I was doing them but cherished as memories now.

Her father, Louis Borders, with his brother Tom, had opened an 800-square-foot used bookstore called Borders Book Shop in Ann Arbor, Michigan, in 1971. Borders Group Inc. grew to become the second of the three largest bookstore chains in the US. It operated 354 superstores under the name Borders Books and Music.

"My dad put every bit of himself into his twenty-five years building Borders," Chris said. *"He focused on truly taking care of both customers and employees. All of these values—hard work, taking care of people, looking at the world from different angles—also became important to me."*

Chris was a graduate of UC Berkeley and Columbia University's joint Master of Business program and, in 2010, launched the independent publishing company Nothing but the Truth (NBTT) to send women's voices out into the world.

NBTT had published two anthologies and two memoirs—one about a woman's journey to pregnancy through freezing her eggs and another about a woman who beat cancer—and a few children's books, including *Stewie BOOM!* penned by Chris.

Chris and I hiked on Crown Road above our homes, and one morning, she shared with me her frustrations with the publishing industry. *"The industry has been reduced to five major publishers controlled by white patriarchal editorial and marketing systems,"* she said as we climbed the hill. *"There isn't a supportive nurturing environment for Black editors that will make publishing truly diverse."*

Her idea was to publish an anthology representing women of color's voices. Chris thought it right to step aside and have a woman of color manage the project. *"Can you co-publish with me?"* she asked.

"Of course, I'd love to."

We began brainstorming so that every aspect of the book would be managed by BIPOC women. Chris gave me an assistant from NBTT, and we sent out calls for submissions through *Poets & Writers* magazine, online sources, and writers' websites. The ad said: *Nothing but the Truth Publishing and editor, Deborah Santana, are looking for essays by women of color for an anthology about topics ranging from relationships, career, community, success, and pain to hoodies and raising children. This anthology will showcase what it means to be a woman of color in America today. The entire book will be written, directed, and edited by women of color, a process we believe does not happen enough in the publishing industry. Essays are to be 800-1,200 words in length.*

We received over 300 submissions and requested additional essays from notable writers. I hired award-winning author and professor Sarah Ladipo Manyika and marketing director Kendall Laidlaw to assist in choosing the most well-written and thematic essays.

At the time, I was enrolled in a course at the San Francisco Theological Seminary: Diploma in the Art of Spiritual Direction to learn to listen deeply to God and be present in every interaction. The readings and class discussions impressed upon students to listen with intuition, knowledge, heart, and soul. We practiced this as we learned each other's names, listening for personal or cultural history in the volume and timbre of each voice, and watched expressions on faces. Each class began with meditation and singing, a chanted opening with the strike of a brass bowl. This communion strengthened my intuitive gleanings outside of class, too, and in a dream, I "heard" the title for the anthology: *All the Women in My Family Sing.* As I read the essays submitted from around the world, it was obvious that a chorus of women's voices was singing out.

Editing took a few months of focused work and legal organizing of contracts, copyrights, and trademarks. I loved every minute working with authors to finetune their essays, planning the cover art, and learning from Chris about the publishing process. My hope was that readers of the anthology would feel bridges to oneness with each writer's story.

● **18**

CEREMONY

I HAD BEEN DIVORCED FOR EIGHT YEARS, living on my own since Angelica left for college, cherishing the peace and solitude of my thoughts and the collaborative work I was engaged with on many projects. My dream of being in a meaningful relationship with a man of high intelligence, who valued health and didn't take drugs, who could see me and hear me, who did not place me in a subordinate position, and who had a spiritual practice to complement mine, had been fulfilled in Carl. I had unspoken rules for any relationship after my marriage: I would not be the homemaker who always prepared dinner, did laundry, and solely maintained the home. I wanted a 50-50 relationship—no outdated roles.

Love is like jazz. There is not just one great song played by one great musician, trio, or band. Jazz is musicians in a group, able to blend the sounds of their instruments, work through chord progressions, improvise, and listen attentively while others play. Like an elegant Wayne Shorter saxophone jazz solo that carries us into celestial galaxies, love could transport us, too.

The night Carl proclaimed he was in love with me, I felt I was in love with him, too. Since we met at Samovar, time had opened us to love—the highest, most revelatory, infectious gathering of two souls. I continued to chant my "look at the big picture" mantra and breathe in gratitude, humility, and love. In through my heart chakra, I breathed; out through my entire being, I exhaled. It amazed me that our desire to be together combined with the ease of being together. Carl said, *"I do not take this time for granted."* Neither did I.

After rehearsals for *Emperor Jones*, or whenever he came to my house at the end of the day, we talked, or if I was already in bed, I got up and sat in the kitchen with him. We were deeply thankful for being brought together in a Divine healing partnership. We talked about God, the presence that was always with us, and Carl shared he struggled with guilt that he hadn't been able to prevent Vonetta's death. I still had remnants of pain from my marriage, and Carl knew I was still healing.

In August, Carl began rehearsal at ACT for *Between Riverside and Crazy*, by playwright Stephen Adly Guirgis, in the role of Walter "Pops" Washington, an ex-cop and widower who was about to lose his rent-controlled apartment in New York City. As he immersed himself in preparation for the role, I withdrew from the Diploma in the Art of Spiritual Listening at the end of the first semester to focus on my commitments with the MoAD board in my role on the Programs Committee, planned my travel to Washington DC, for the Smithsonian National Board meetings, and to work on the book of poetry I was creating at the San Francisco Center for the Book. In this endeavor, with the supervision of Mary Risala Laird, I typeset each word. She patiently showed me how to set the letters on the large press, tighten the rollers, and load the paper. The machine was so large, I had to run along while I turned the crank, allowing the ink to spread. One of my poems was about Carl:

Celestial Storm

My sweet gardener Antonio brought new plants for beneath the
camelias at the bottom of the stairs leading to my front door.
He put his hands into the soil & replaced irrigation lines, black
rubber tubing holding beads of precious water that
we did not take for granted now.
He buried roots, knowing with confidence that
what he planted would grow.
I was having a crisis of not knowing if my hands were planting
roots in you, of missing the touch of the rich, dark soil of you,
of wanting to place my body on yours & feel the
warm stickiness of your skin.
I was having a crisis of wondering when you would let go of what was,
Even though I knew you were exactly in the center of you.
We were traveling in the membrane of a celestial storm
of stars and meteors flashing through all time,
exploding in a guided essence of beauty & rhythm.
Did you know that our hearts beat 100,000 times each day?
That was where I was—
In the beat of your heart, the echoes of your feet planting firmly on
the sidewalk, using forty muscles to take a single step.

Carl and I met for dinner at one of our favorite Marin restaurants, Tamalpie, and stuffed ourselves with aromatic Neapolitan-style pizza and salads with butter lettuce, avocado, and kale.

"*Can we talk about our goals?*" he asked.

I looked up, attentive for his next words. "*You are a big part of my goals,*" he continued. I wiped my mouth with my napkin, sensing he was going to reveal something significant. "*I would like to be married,*" he said.

I began to smile. "*Oh! I knew I wanted to marry you a while ago,*" I laughed. He reached over and rubbed his hand across my cheek. I was a little taken aback that I could be so open and honest with this man. We were comfortable together and stared into each other's eyes as if no one else was eating beside us in the noisy Mill Valley restaurant. We had a waiter take a photo of us standing together to memorialize the night, but that was for me because I knew Carl had already memorized it.

My glee was dampened a bit when I told Kitsaun about our engagement. *"Are you sure? Why do you have to get married?"* she asked, her brow furrowed. She and Gregory had been together eighteen years, and she never wanted to marry.

I never felt an ounce of fear about marrying again. LaTanya brought us to this ultimate destination of love through her vision of Carl and me. I told my sister, *"I like committing to share life with another person. I guess we're just the marrying kind."* She withheld any further thoughts, but I could feel her disapproval, or maybe she wanted to protect me in some way.

Carl and I decided to tell our children. We wanted their blessings.

Angelica said, *"If that makes you happy, Mom, I'm happy."*

Stella was surprised. *"Wow, Mom. Congratulations!"*

Carl said, *"I'm going to Los Angeles to tell Brandon. And I will ask Salvador for his permission to marry you."*

I agreed that was a perfect offering to make to my son—a little old fashioned but respectful for the only other man in my family. I wished I could call Mom. I missed talking with her, sharing my experiences, and listening to her wise responses. I wondered what she would say. She always wanted the best for me, and I believed my happiness would be proof that this was good.

Once we had our children's blessings, I began planning. My first marriage had taken place in my Uncle U.S.'s living room with Mom and Dad, Kitsaun, and Aunt Bitsy as our only guests. For the upcoming nuptials, I wanted an elegant room, candles all around, and our family and friends with us.

Carl and I sat in my family room, fire blazing, eyes glowing with affection, and I asked him, *"Why don't you move in? We'll be married in four months."*

His voice was deep. *"Deborah Sara, there is nothing I'd like more."*

We agreed to wed eight months after we met for tea at Samovar—I felt drawn to this but was also amenable to the one-year mark of April 30.

We thought it through and knew we couldn't count on Carl's schedule being free in April, so December 30 it was.

I considered this day uniquely significant because the close of 2015 brought a wide-open light-filled promise for 2016. It felt perfect—our families would be with us, at the location we had chosen, the Carneros Inn in Napa. Our invitation list was small, and LaTanya and Sam's schedules allowed them to come. Carl called our union a "grand elopement." He mentioned the large number of people at his wedding to Vonetta and that she had arrived an hour and a half late. I sensed he was still processing that loss, and I trusted he would honor our love in the present.

On our wedding eve, we scheduled an informal pizza night in Carneros Home #3 with outdoor heaters and a firepit warming Stella and her boyfriend, Paul; Angelica; Carl's son, Brandon; Salvador and Megan; my niece Chloe; and cousins and friends—the firelight dancing an amber glow on their faces, and laughter peeling from their lips.

Carl and Salvador picked up pizzas from Azzurro: pepperoni, funghi, verde, White Lightning, and margherita. I made a large mixed green salad, and we had wine from Brown Estate Winery that Stella picked up. Carl said a prayer before our meal. Being together consecrated the joining of our families, and we talked and laughed in celebration. I prayed tomorrow would be even more special as Carl and I proclaimed our vows of love before cherished family and friends.

I was saying yes to every moment.

———

At nine am on December 30, 2015, it was 37 degrees outside, the air icy and crisp. Carl and I visited the hotel gym and worked out, with no sign of our children, who had probably stayed up extremely late talking and enjoying the wine. We walked to Boon Fly Cafe for breakfast, where LaTanya and Sam had arrived and sat at the counter. LaTanya was wrapped in a black cashmere shawl. She smiled, *"I was right about you two."*

I gave her a hug and reminded her of our last meeting in New York when Stella and I had attended *A Raisin in the Sun* at the Ethel Barrymore

Theatre. "*I couldn't get your performance out of my mind for weeks. You were remarkable, my friend. It was a work of art.*"

"*I am so glad you and Stella came,*" she said.

The ceremony was everything I dreamed of. The pastor invoked Spirit before the recitation of our vows. My vows stated exactly what I was feeling: "*In my heart, I always knew it would be like this: In one predestined, miraculous moment, I would meet you—a man who carries the light of a thousand stars, who sees into my heart and cherishes the essence of my being. I love you, Carl Winston, with every cell.*"

We walked to the Hilltop Room, which was bathed in amber candlelight, with bouquets of pink roses, white amaryllis, and sage on each table. The room shimmered with the glow of Carl's and my love as the DJ began playing our songs and we had our first dance. Spirit had blessed us with a meaningful day of commitment to our souls' connection.

19

CENTRAL TO THE AMERICAN STORY

As the world's largest museum complex, the Smithsonian is a web of about 6,500 employees, curators, researchers, security teams, food providers, scholars, and scientists. Each one brings expertise in their specific area to serve in the positions for which they have been hired. More than 4.3 million people participate in their educational programs.

It's not widely known that the Institution was gifted to America by James Smithson, an Oxford-educated Englishman, chemist, and mineralogist who had never traveled to the country he donated over £500,000 to—until he was buried in a crypt in the Castle. Although Smithson's father was a duke, he had trouble gaining respect in English society because his parents never married, so he was seen as an outcast. The Smithsonian Institution Archives held the position that Smithson wanted to build a legacy outside his home country because of this rejection. Congress appointed a board of regents to oversee the funds. True to the political and cultural behaviors of the time, the governance was comprised solely of white males.

The National Board of Directors participates in decisions made by individual Smithsonian directors, curators, and senior staff. However, every Smithsonian Museum is unique, with its own board of directors, not under the direction of the National Board. Each has its own architecture, unique history, and educational offerings. Each offers internships and fellowships, and education is at the forefront of every endeavor.

I quickly learned that the Smithsonian's many initiatives would provide an opportunity to expand my giving. My hunger to learn as much as possible drove my involvement. My first impression of Washington, DC, the Smithsonian Institution, and the pageantry of events for the National Board of Directors was that there were staggering amounts of art and antiquities in the collections and formalities not often experienced in my younger state of California.

I was asked to become a donor for the newest museum, the Smithsonian National Museum of African American History and Culture (NMAAHC). I was thrilled and said yes. As it turns out, I was the first founding donor from California, which made me burst with pride. This museum would be a "first of all firsts," more than twelve years in the making since an act of Congress established its creation, and ninety-nine years since the idea was introduced legislatively.

Its five-acre location on the National Mall looked across the north lawn to the Washington Monument; to the east was the US Capitol, seat of the nation's legislature; to the south and west were monuments and memorials to Thomas Jefferson, Martin Luther King Jr., Abraham Lincoln, and George Washington. On my first visit, I donned a yellow hard hat, just as I had on my first visit to MoAD and joined a tour. I visited Lonnie Bunch, founding director of the project, whose credentials made me bow with respect. A historian, educator, and author, Lonnie had been part of the core team that built the California African American Museum in Los Angeles and oversaw the transformation of the Chicago Historical Society.

Lonnie was gracious and generous with his time. "*I want this museum to make America better,*" he said. "*I traveled to small towns and into people's basements and attics to see artifacts from our history. Everyone willingly donated their personal treasure to the museum.*" He made me feel I was an important part of this momentous building campaign with my contribution as a founding donor.

In September 2016, everyone who contributed to the building of the museum, along with all who wanted to celebrate the festivities, received invitations to the opening ceremonies of NMAAHC. Some of us were also included in a reception at the White House with a formal invitation from President and Mrs. Obama.

I had never been interested in visiting the White House, as I had never thought of it as the hallowed place of "inclusion and belonging" that it touted itself to be. Historical records stated that construction began in 1792 with the labor of enslaved and free African Americans, and—as described in Jesse Holland's book *Black Men Built the Capitol: Discovering African-American History In and Around Washington, DC*—*"Slaves helped to dig the building's foundation. Slaves were also used at Virginia quarries to chop stone out of the ground for the walls of the building and elsewhere to dig clay for bricks and saw timber for as little as thirteen cents a day—wages that were most likely pocketed by their masters."* In spite of this history, I felt I couldn't pass up this opportunity, so Carl and I traveled together to the events.

Standing in line at the southwest entrance of the White House for the president's reception, I saw C.T. Vivian ahead of me. Slender and wearing a dark suit, the minister, author, and close friend of Martin Luther King Jr. exuded a strength of knowledge in his carriage. I watched his curved, ninety-two-year-old body and was honored to be close to him. He joined us in the line outside with no special treatment, although I thought he deserved it. The fact that he blended in showed just how important that day was. There were many notable people in attendance.

Inside the White House, we were relatively free to roam. I stood in the State Dining Room before glass cabinets with State Dinner Service China: President Obama's porcelain made by Pickard China in Illinois and President John F. Kennedy's made by Morgantown Glassware Guild of Morgantown, West Virginia, which featured a single gold rim around white plates. In the Green Room parlor, I had my photo taken against a green silk wall, with a gilded oval mirror at my side reflecting a glass chandelier and a painting by Henry Ossawa Tanner, *Sand Dunes at Sunset, Atlantic City (1885)*.

There must have been 300 people in the rooms and hallways, their laughter and loud voices echoing. Wearing shades of purple, a choir huddled in Cross Hall singing "Grateful" by Hezekiah Walker, their voices earnest and lovely. Chills ran through my body, feeling the meaning of the gospel song—the chord changes and words expressing how I felt to be a part of this monumental opening.

I saw Quincy Jones in his wheelchair and gave him the biggest hug; senator John Lewis was walking down the hall just a few feet away. I was so fortunate to be in the presence of giving, life-changing humans who had done so much for equality and righting the wrongs of this country. President Obama and Michelle welcomed Lonnie to a small stage in the hallway under the seal of the president of the United States, with twelve-foot flags flanking the open doors behind. *"We're here just to acknowledge what an extraordinary achievement has been accomplished by Mr. Lonnie Bunch and everybody who helped make this day possible . . . When Lonnie first came here from Chicago to start work on this museum a decade ago, he could not even find somebody to give him a key to his office."* There was laughter in the audience. *"Nobody had heard of this museum. And now you cannot miss it—a breathtaking new building right in the heart of the National Mall. And that is what we call progress. It could not have been done without the persistence, the wisdom, the dedication, the savvy, the ability to make people feel guilty—the begging, the deal-making, and just the general street smarts of Lonnie and his entire team. So please give him a big round of applause for all the work that he has done."*

And applaud we did, along with sending out a few hoots and whistles, while Lonnie stood, head bowed, accepting our thanks.

Saturday, September 24, the dedication ceremony outside the grounds of the museum, with hosts President Barack Obama, First Lady Michelle Obama, Lonnie Bunch, former President George Bush, and former First Lady Laura Bush was a once-in-a-lifetime fête. Carl and I were joined by Kitsaun and Gregory, my niece Kelli, and her husband, Jack. LaTanya and Sam had become founding donors as well and were in seats near us. Seven thousand people were in rows of white chairs with thousands more sitting on the lawns. More than 100,000 people had become members of the museum, paying a minimum of $25 to join—exceptional participation before the museum even opened.

"African-American history is not somehow separate from the American story. It is not the underside of the American story. It is central to the American story," Obama said of the 36,000 artifacts inside the 400,000-square-foot museum. John Lewis, Oprah Winfrey, Will Smith, Supreme Court Chief Justice John G. Roberts Jr., and former President George W. Bush gave speeches. I was transfixed by each speaker's words, feeling a luminous joy that the mission to launch this museum had come to fruition and I had played a small role. As John Lewis, emotional and pure, said, *"This place is more than a building. It is a dream come true."*

Stevie Wonder was guided onstage. *"I was born blind, but I was blessed with inner vision. Inner vision sees what we all know and feel, and what I know and feel is that we must come together . . . all of the hatred trying to divide the United States of America cannot go on. Remember our strength, remember our courage."* He sang, "Where Is Our Love Song?" Lonnie and John Lewis faced him, and Michelle swayed and smiled. It was a song of love.

Patti LaBelle floated onto the stage wearing pale pink and gave a powerful rendition of "A Change Is Gonna Come." I was on the wave with her, sailing forward in freedom. People around me shed tears at the tribute to change being displayed on the National Mall.

Lonnie Bunch again stood at the mic: *"Today, a dream too long deferred is a dream no longer. What a grand and glorious day to open a museum that will not just tell of a people's journey but also of a nation's story that would help all Americans realize how much they've been shaped, informed, and made better by the African-American experience."*

The days of celebration in 2016 left me filled beyond anything I had expected when I agreed to be a founding donor. I hadn't foreseen the ancestors I would feel standing with me in the White House and on the grounds and in the concourses of the museum. I could not have imagined how the chords and words of the song "Grateful" would place me in the choir of my family church, arms raised in praise, feeling the victory of the president, first lady, Lonnie Bunch, and all the workers and donors. It was a privilege to have celebrated with friends and icons of the monument to liberation—a thrilling communion, a sacred sharing of the legacies of my family and millions of Black people.

20

THE WOMEN'S MARCH

Chris Bronstein's and my intention to publish our anthology of women of color's voices was never more important than after the November 2016 presidential election. The results resoundingly shocked me, my friends, my family, and the Democratic Party. Although millions of people voted to choose the new president, only 54.8 percent of the eligible population cast ballots.

Hillary Clinton lost the opportunity to become the first woman president of the United States by 80,000 votes in three states. We later found out that Russia had played a significant role in spreading false information and damaging claims about Clinton that affected voters' confidence in her. And, just like that, a New York businessman with despicable morals became the 45th leader of this country.

The night of election returns, Carl and I crawled into bed depressed and defeated. How could intelligent, rational people vote for a misogynist who aligned his politics with white supremacists, cheating, corruption, and Russian anti-American intelligence? *All the Women in My Family Sing* became my anthem for equality.

The day after the election, Teresa Shook, a grandmother living in Hawaii, posted on Facebook an idea for a march on Washington, DC, before inauguration day. Thousands knitted or crocheted pink "pussy" hats in protest of the newly inaugurated president's vulgar and denigrating language caught off camera from a 2005 interview when he boasted, *"When you're a star . . . you can do anything . . . Grab 'em by the pussy. You can do anything."*

I purchased my hat online and found a note inside written by a man who had knit the hat in support of women. Kitsaun and I flew to Washington, DC, to participate in the Women's March on January 21, 2017. The day before, we participated in the Nonviolence and Active Bystander Intervention Training at Washington City Church of the Brethren. It was sponsored by *Sojourners Magazine* to "learn and share words and tactics for de-escalating conflict."

Many of us who worked to further the rights and equal opportunities for women, people of color, the LGBTQI+ community, and persons with disabilities felt a need to plan how to protect ourselves if we were targeted in aggressive or violent ways in the new regime of hatred and bolder-than-ever racism. The workshop was informational, and being in the presence of other activists was soothing. We were taught ways to create a safe space in combative encounters with suggestions to use inclusive language and active listening, have mutual respect, admit when you don't know, assume the best, and step up to talk, step back to listen. I left the workshop ready to be an active bystander if I saw violence.

The morning of the Women's March, DC, the weather was a mild 48 degrees—a temperature my California blood could handle. We boarded the subway to meet our friend Sharon Gelman on the stairs of the Library of Congress. Women in pink pussy hats were buying tickets. *"Hello, sisters!"* one woman said to us. *"Where are you from?"*

"California," I answered. Whoops and laughter went up. *"We're a group of mothers from Oregon. We knit our hats."*

A woman asked, *"Do you have an extra?"*

"Yes. It's small, but I think it will fit you."

The dark-haired woman said, *"Thank you. I am a journalist from* Elle *magazine, France. I am here to write about the march."*

At each Metro stop, women pushed onto the train holding signs of protest. A cacophonous layer of chanting and clapping echoed all around.

Sayings on posters were:

- Respect existence or expect resistance

- Mother Nature is a woman too. Climate change is real.

- Make America think again!

- Love trumps hate

- John Lewis For President

- Let's change history, not repeat it

- Not my President / Nyet my President!

- Nasty women!

- My uterus, my business

- No human is illegal

- You can't comb over misogyny

- A nation is not defeated until the hearts of its women are on the ground

- Women's rights are not up for grabs!

- Men of quality do not fear equality

I expected a powerful gathering of righteously angry women, and, exiting the subway, Kitsaun and I were swept into the wave of protestors—women, yes, but men and children too. People flooded the streets, many in historical costumes of suffragettes and famous women icons. It was a miracle we found Sharon on the steps of the granite building with its golden dome. We screamed and walked into each other's arms and followed Sharon to find a place to stand to listen to the speakers.

Activists lined up behind the outdoor stage, much like the stages of music concerts. But attendance here was motivated by the voices of powerful women.

Linda Sarsour, one of the national co-chairs for the Women's March on Washington, spoke: *"I stand here before you, unapologetically Muslim*

American . . . unapologetically Palestinian American . . . unapologetically from Brooklyn, New York . . . Sisters and brothers, you are what democracy looks like . . . I will respect the presidency, but I will not respect this president of the United States of America. . . I will not respect an administration that won an election on the backs of Muslims and black people and undocumented people and Mexicans and people with disabilities and on the backs of women."

Actor America Ferrera stepped up: *"The president is not America. His cabinet is not America. Congress is not America. We are America. And we are here to stay. We will not go from being a nation of immigrants to a nation of ignorance."*

Worldwide respected professor, activist, and leader Angela Davis shouted, *"The freedom and struggles of Black people that have shaped the very nature of this country's history cannot be deleted with the sweep of a hand . . . Spreading xenophobia, hurling accusations of murder and rape, and building walls will not erase history."*

Then we all began walking down Independence Avenue, a hundred people wide, part of a crowd that was estimated to have grown to 600,000. We were euphoric in our chanting, *"This is what democracy looks like!"* We shouted until our voices gave out.

After the march—feet tired, throats raw, hearts wide open—Kitsaun and I stopped at a restaurant to have dinner, satisfied that the day had been a massive success. There had been very few police on the streets. *"Do you think the new administration miscalculated the number of people who would attend?"* I asked Kitsaun as we ate.

"Or they wanted us to run over ourselves in chaos and anarchy," she answered. *"We showed them."*

We had preached, walked, carried signs, and gathered in peace to protest the incoming executive branch, including drawing more participants than the presidential swearing-in ceremony the day before. We felt triumphant.

Returning home to finish my work on the anthology became my contribution to a solidarity among women who refused to be silenced. We requested and were granted permission to use America Ferrera's speech from the Women's March in the book and received essays from my friend Marian Wright Edelman, CEO of the Children's Defense Fund; my friend Lalita Tademy; author Samina Ali; and *Queen Sugar*'s author, Natalie Baszile. The book received endorsements from Isabel Allende, Alfre Woodard, and Henry Louis Gates Jr., among others.

The voices in our anthology were a call to resist the boundaries inflicted on us by a patriarchal, misogynistic system of oppression. We joined the worldwide protests of women from every ethnic and socio-economic background against inequality and decades of workplace and domestic abuse. Each essay asked us to expand our minds and have the courage to change the future.

Our writers of color stepped onto a stage that illuminated the diversity and complexity of women's experiences. Writer Jack Shea in the *Martha's Vineyard Times* referenced my foreword when he reviewed the anthology:

"Santana offers a perspective in her introduction that informs the read. She points out that more than 99 percent of DNA, shared by all human beings, is exactly the same. Not similar, the same. The other 1 percent, the part that makes each of us unique—hair, skin, tall, short, wide, or thin, comes from our parents. We have made an obvious mess of that 1 percent for centuries here. The demagogues have fanned the 1 percent into a societal crisis in America. Race is the most obvious marker of our social divide, but they highlight ethnicity, gender, regional cultures, even accents, as unacceptable differences that ought to be used to prejudge us."

The project brought Chris and me closer than ever as we attended book events with the authors and basked in their life experiences through their words. At many of the readings, audience members cried, hearing stories that reflected their own. It was an extraordinary opportunity to engage with women of diverse cultures who lit up the world with courage. Every reading was a celebration, every essay a transmission of life beyond outdated perceptions of what it meant to be human.

Capturing how lives had been affected in that divisive and dangerous time, the writers in *All the Women in My Family Sing* showed us a better way to find home. Together.

———

I continued to meet women I felt solidarity with in working to
eradicate injustice and make a difference in the state of the world. I had
met Australian actress Viva Bianca when she attended a fundraiser I held
for Daraja Academy in Los Angeles, and I supported her work to finish a
documentary, *Milkshake Girls,* about a young woman who was abducted
and sold into child slavery. Viva invited me to sign on as an executive
producer on a film she was producing and directing about youth climate
activism and student climate strikes that were happening across the globe.
Standing five feet nine, Viva possessed the courage and mental strength
of a gladiator.

One of the leads of our documentary was Tokata Iron Eyes, a Lakota
environmental activist and Indigenous student leader. I had the privilege
to sit in when Viva interviewed her in a Los Angeles studio. She talked
about her mother, pediatrician and environmental activist, Sara Jumping
Eagle, and how her activism influenced Tokata's passion to fight for land
back and oppose the construction of the Dakota Access Pipeline. Tokata
said, *"When Indigenous people are talking about the climate crisis, we are
[asking] how are we going to protect this world and our own stories and ways
of knowing and being for our children and our children's children?"*

Viva had two children aged one and three when she began filming. *"I
love my children so much,"* she told me. *"How do I look them in the eye when
I know that their futures are so at risk because of the inaction of our leaders?"*
This question fueled her to travel to New York, Seattle, Minneapolis, and
Los Angeles to interview the four key players who had committed their
young lives to climate activism.

Activist Jamie Margolin, founder of Zero Hour, said, *"Climate change
affects women more than men. 80% of those affected are women."* Jamie, who
was fully engaged in protests in Seattle, added, *"People call us Generation
Z as if we are the last generation. But we are not. We refuse to be the last letter
in the alphabet. So, today I announce before the whole country that we are
Generation GND. The generation of the Green New Deal."*

Greta Thunberg was a leader of this youth movement and had begun
skipping school on Fridays to protest outside of the Swedish Parliament
with a sign that read, "Strike for the Climate." This strike became known

as #FridaysForFuture, and, thanks to social media, teenagers and adults in hundreds of cities and towns all over the world joined her.

Isra Hirsi was just sixteen when she campaigned with the group she cofounded: US Youth Climate Strikes.

Jesús Villalba, just seventeen, proclaimed simply, *"I guess it is everyone's wish not to die,"* as the reason he fought for issues of climate equity.

The documentary was shot on iPhones, some generously donated to us by Lisa Jackson at Apple. As I had with the Daraja documentaries I produced, I participated in watching and commenting on final edits. When we locked film, the last version gave me chills, the voices of these activists strong and fearless. The village of women I belong to is a brave circle of truth warriors.

21

INCOMPATIBLE SOFTWARE

Carl and I assiduously wrote together every morning we were together. We sat at the kitchen table, orange linen napkins folded into rectangles, our notebooks in front of us. I sat high on my chair, feet crossed at my ankles. Through the wall-wide window, houses down the hill were shrouded in live oak and buckeye trees, filtering the sun's light. Coltrane's notes proffered from his alto sax, scaling spiritual realms only he could express, and Carl and I wrote while communing in the constellation of his music. Could I lay my bones, skin, limbs, and heart on the page to express the ethos of who I am? Coltrane took a breath, and I relaxed. My words touched paper as his fingers touched keys, and his jazz riffs began again.

Love is one of the most ecstatic experiences to enjoy. Romance is filled with bliss and euphoria, and those of us who are fortunate enough to be in romantic relationships cherish that feeling in our bodies. Carl and I had fallen into love easily, with abandon. We had known the beauty of love with our first spouses and were joyously surprised to feel it again. We walked into a thrilling connection that revived us both.

John Kim, licensed marriage and family therapist, wrote in *Psychology Today*: "*You don't fall in love. You discover it. Then it's built . . . You fall in lust. You fall in infatuation. You fall in amazing chemistry and connection. You fall in hot sex. But you don't fall in love. Love is discovered."*

Five months after our union, Carl was starring in the play *Red Velvet* about actor Ira Aldridge at the San Francisco Playhouse. I watched him inhabit the character of a trailblazer who was the first Black actor to step onto a London stage in the 1820s, and his performance was captivating. I loved watching his presence grow on the stage as he proclaimed, *"Unfortunately, money does not guarantee character."* I gleaned some of the intricacies of acting through watching him prepare, rehearse, and perform, and my respect for actors grew.

When the play ended, Carl and I flew to Ireland to tour a land that is part of my ancestry. My research showed my European origins were 37 percent English and Northwestern European, 13 percent Scottish, and 2 percent Welsh. The trip was planned by a tour company, and we arrived in Dublin, then traveled to Killarney, Ring of Kerry, and ended our stay at Dromoland Castle on the far west coast in County Clare. I had never lodged in a castle, and Dromoland was as dramatic and majestic as I imagined. The baronial estate was made of dark blue limestone with four castellated turrets, and its interior design was formal, with furnishings covered with velvet and chintz. It was a bit too prim and proper for my tastes, but everyone we met was kind and welcoming. We saw little of the 500 acres the castle owned, but I loved most the beech, oak, and sycamore trees stretching skyward. Carl played golf in the pouring rain, and we scheduled two hours with a falconry instructor. Hawks had been my animal totem since my divorce. They have flown into my garden, spread their wings over my car, and rested on lamp posts whenever I needed comfort or guidance. They remind me to look at the big picture and not drown in trivial details or fears. Although falcons are smaller in size, they are equally impressive in beauty and power.

We walked to the woodlands with rolling grasses and met our guide. He held the bird on his gloved arm, his beautiful walnut-brown feathers with sunset hues on his back, white tail feathers, and a yellow beak. I donned the black leather glove on my left hand and arm, and when the instructor placed the bird on my arm, I was surprised at how light it was. *"What does she weigh?"* I asked.

"Most falcons weigh about one and a half pounds, the largest being two and a half pounds."

Carl said, *"That's what allows them to fly so fast."*

We learned their leg bones were hollow, and they were fed raw chicken that the trainers cut up daily. The trainer gave the bird a signal and he flew off into the trees. I could hardly see him in the distance until he began his return and headed for my gloved arm. I giggled audibly at the thrill of having this totem fly to me, pushing my arm back as she landed.

When we returned to California, I traveled to Belize on a service trip with Ambassador Attallah Shabazz, the eldest daughter of Dr. Betty Shabazz and Malcolm X. A diplomat, actor, producer, and philanthropist, she was appointed ambassador to Belize in 2002. She is stately, warm, intelligent, and fun. As ambassador, her mission is to foster diplomatic relations between cultures—and she succeeded with our delegation of eight women. We met with members of the Garifuna people who sang songs with conga drums and maracas as accompaniment. While they played, we danced on a dusty floor, weaving around the room. I visited a baboon sanctuary, walking over two rivers with brownish green water. My guide, Geraldine, used her voice to call the baboons, *"Come boys, come,"* before she issued a guttural bark. The baboons swung through the trees in response. Ambassador Shabazz took us to visit women in the Belize Central Prison where we painted large tires to place in the garden as flower planters. The inmates talked with us about their lives there, and the cement room we sat in was as bare as any I'd seen. Our time with Ambassador Shabazz connected us with Belizean life and Indigenous traditions that were new to me.

In June 2018, Carl was filming *Supergirl* in Vancouver, and I rented an apartment in Los Angeles, awaiting the birth of Salvador and Megan's baby. Furnishings were leased, and new bedding and dishes were purchased to facilitate me traveling from Marin to Sherman Oaks once a month to be an on-site grandmother.

I moved into the third-floor domicile with no expectations. I had not lived near Salvador in fifteen years, and it was wonderful to be close to him again. I adjusted to the roar and hum of cars driving down Moorpark in front of the apartment but missed my hikes on Mount Tamalpais's trails with tall redwoods, wild mushrooms, columbine, and live oak trees.

The day my first grandchild, Stevie, was born, there were complications in his little body. Salvador and Megan were rushed with him to another hospital where he stayed in the NICU for two and a half months. I remained in the Los Angeles apartment without returning to Marin. Each morning, I awakened early and went on hikes to Fryman Canyon or around neighboring environs. It wasn't peaceful like my Marin hikes, but I felt relief and solace being near Salvador during this stressful time. Afternoons I visited Stevie in the hospital, praying for his perfect healing and for Salvador and Megan. We spoke softly in Stevie's room, telling him, "*We love you, Stevie. Spirit loves you.*" I printed out an affirmation and taped it to the wall above his crib:

Life harmonizes Stevie's body so that it is revitalized and manifests perfection in every cell, organ, and function. Stevie's whole being manifests the life, love, peace, harmony, strength, and joy of the Spirit that dwells within him.

Angelica, Stella, Kitsaun, and Gregory visited, touching Stevie's tiny hand.

My strides followed my own rhythm, with my days centered on Stevie. Carl visited for a few days, but I felt removed, as if he were a stranger. We hadn't been together very much, and I now saw differences in who we were, rather than the romantic illusion of eternal oneness I initially felt. Stevie's fight for life changed my focus from my fulfillment to his survival. Every day I sat at my small altar intoning healing words as I lifted my face to the omnipotent Divine energy, pleading for Stevie's life to continue. I started to feel Carl pull away as my attention on our marriage shifted to Stevie. We had enjoyed discovering each other, and I had believed the magical feelings would last the rest of our lives, but the carefree moments of adoring each other were diminishing as Stevie became the center of my days. Carl was absorbed in reading, writing a play about James Baldwin, which we both considered important, exercising, and playing golf with friends.

———

THE IMPRINT OF CARL EMBOSSED ON MY HEART WAS FADING. Had I been caught in the excitement of meeting a magnificent man and not realized it was the elation of early dating? Now, I craved my own space. It was like our software systems were no longer compatible—just like that.

John Kim also wrote: "*Possible hurt is always the buy-in to discovering love. There's no way around that.*"

I was the one who fell off the love bike. In my small apartment, I discovered solitude, and I felt an urge to be alone.

In *The Poets Laureate Anthology*, Charles Simic wrote that it was a poet's responsibility to bear witness and record his or her reactions to a historical moment so that there was an alternative narrative to the often-distorting propaganda written for or by politicians. "*The poet, like anyone else, is part of history, but he or she ought to be the conscious part. That's the ideal . . .*"

To write my narrative, I had to listen—not only to words but to vibrations in my body telling me the truth of my rousing emotions. When I went to my first workshop with Natalie Goldberg in 1996, I didn't have my own essence. I wasn't aware of this, but she later told me, "*You appeared gray when we first met.*" I was a noncolor, not emitting a personal aura. I had been a representative of Carlos's life, his music, his world. As I began writing my story, I claimed my individuality and blossomed into a fuller person, a hue of assorted colors.

Now I had morphed again, melding myself with Carl. Was I becoming colorless again?

I was reading the book, *Listen Here!* by Megan McKenna, and paid much more attention to listening than I had before. I heard air being pushed beneath crows' wings as I walked trails and cherished the whooshing flap. Wings produced a powerful sound if you were quiet enough and listened.

I watched a video of a Dine woman, Pat McCabe, who had an experience with water flowing up from the ground under her home. She began to speak to the water, asking it to please not rise near her storage shed as everything would be destroyed. "*Please,*" she said, "*do not flow to my neighbors' as they are distressed, they will have damage to their gardens.*" She paused. Her chest rose under the black blouse she wore. "*It makes me* cry," she said, "*because I heard the water respond in my heart. Water is life; water is sacred.*" She had to leave her home for three weeks, and when she returned, the flowing water had created a fork in its path, moving around the areas she had asked it to. The water listened.

Similarly, I was listening to my heart. I heard, "*Be centered in wholeness. Be content. Let only your light guide you.*"

Stevie was released from the NICU and went home. I flew to New York to visit Stella. I walked two miles through Manhattan to an appointment with an acupuncturist. He inserted needles into my skin at various meridians along my body to stimulate my central nervous system, and I hoped, to heal the migraines I had been experiencing.

I started my walk back to Stella's when Carl called. Seeing a bench in the center of honking cars and hundreds of pedestrians, I sat. "*Hi,*" I said.

"*When are you coming back?*" he asked.

I had thought about our marriage, about wanting to continue living on my own. Through tears, I told him, "*I'm going to stay in LA. It isn't that I don't love you. I just need to be on my own again. I think you should move out.*"

Those were difficult words to say, but Stevie's life had made me strong enough to do what was best for me. Carl was hurt and angry—and not without reason. He sputtered, "*Why? What happened?*"

I responded, "*I'm not sure, but I have changed.*"

I closed my eyes and breathed. After a long pause, he said, "*I will do as you wish, Deborah Sara. On the first day we met, I told myself that even if the only thing we had was a deep friendship, I would be very happy.*"

I cried, "*Thank you.*"

Was I crazy? I listened to my heart. She said that I must be grateful for the mess of me and my choices, and for beginning again in the purity of my soul.

New York was the best place to shed tears in public. No one notices you.

I sat in the cacophony, the bench hard under my body. Warm steam from subway vents wafted onto my skin, smelling like the city's underground systems of rails and pulleys. This smell had always been comforting to me—telling me New York would always be New York. Nearby, a musician played a wooden lute; another sat on a *cajon*, playing rhythm. Vendors sold bright yellow "I Love New York" t-shirts. I felt lighter, freed by speaking my truth to Carl. I hadn't always had the courage to choose myself, but I had learned there was no other way.

I rose to walk back to my hotel, mothers pushing strollers in front of me, pigeons scuttling along the sidewalk pecking at crumbs. Trees were still in full bloom; some flecked with autumn leaves in golds and reds. Two young men sat on folding chairs playing chess on a card table. Whole Foods' windows were covered in advertisements, and I stopped inside to buy a salad, smiling at the woman behind the salad bar who kindly smiled back.

Carl was a loving port of call. I knew, as I did when I left Carlos, that I was whole within myself, and I never wanted to stagnate or settle in a relationship. I could no longer subordinate or abandon myself. I was motivated to invent, create, challenge my mind, and soar.

22

TO COURAGE

I BEGAN ATTENDING A CHURCH in mid-Wilshire, where the pastor was part metaphysical teacher, part holiness orator. I felt good in the service, especially uplifted by the music. My Sunday afternoons were carved out of stillness. Other families gathered in their homes, sharing a meal, as we had when my children were living at home. The playgrounds near my apartment were filled with children on swings screaming joyfully. Sometimes I visited with Salvador and his family but was often by myself. The apartment I had rented was small, and, in my heart, I knew I wasn't going to return to Marin. I continued to plan my future and drove through neighborhoods close to Salvador, looking at houses. I wanted to be near Stevie. Touring a few open houses, I found one that was large enough for the children to visit but cozy enough for me to live alone. The garden was lush with a tall Chinese elm, a Western sycamore, and a red fuchsia bush, with room for me to plant roses and a lemon bush. I put my Marin home on the market and made an offer on the new house. It was meant to be because both houses closed escrow on the same day—my dad's birthday.

Moving into my new home and new city, the work I did with Bay Area nonprofits kept my connections there alive. One of the nonprofits I was involved with was Futures Without Violence and their interactive program, The Courage Museum. In the Presidio National Park, the museum would engage visitors in a learning journey toward making a world in which violence was not an inevitable part of the human experience. I joined with the staff, partners, and curators at meetings in person and on Zoom to shape the vision and development of programs and exhibitions.

Courage empowers us to move forward and claim the truth of our existence: we are more than what we have experienced. We are slivers of divine life; we are part of each other. In concentrating on my personal growth, I expanded my relationship with Spirit, being mindful of all life encounters. I wanted my inner life to be balanced with my outer life and started having Reiki sessions. Reiki is an attunement, its roots in an ancient Japanese system of moving energy, or Chi—spiritual consciousness—through the body. I signed up to study with a practitioner who guided me through the first two levels of training. In her spacious apartment, she said, *"Be willing to focus on the present moment and relinquish attachment to the past or future. When you focus on what is happening right here, you have clarity and personal power."* She poured us cups of hot tea and explained that Reiki brought serenity. *"Let your heart intelligence be your guide."*

She gave me a session where she gently placed her hands on meridians, or energy points, on my body, clearing out any stress. Afterward, she stood behind me as I sat in a chair with my eyes closed. I heard the movement of her hands up and down my back; she was giving me the attunement that joined me with the lineage of Reiki masters. My mind sensed a strong energy as she initiated me, activating Reiki. I breathed in this new clearing and balance in my chakras. I was reminded that life was sacred and not mine to control. My responsibility was to feel Spirit, align with Divine guidance, and surrender my life to God's love.

There are many Reiki practitioners in Los Angeles, and I found another master to attune me to the third level. She asked my intention before my session. Breathing deeply, I asked, *"Can you please send cleansing energy to any areas of my body holding trauma?"*

I lay on her massage table, closed my eyes, and felt I was floating on a sun-kissed cumulus cloud, feeling the softness of God's light around me. Her hands radiated heat on the sides of my head as Reiki began to flow. When the session was over, I rose from the table filled with gratitude. My life was engulfed in healing energy as never before.

I visited my Reiki teacher's circles with other practitioners, and we gave each other energizing Reiki treatments. We were invited into private homes, and there was no hierarchical structure—those who had practiced Reiki for ten years sat humbly beside those of us who had just begun. That's the beauty and generosity of this community. Each Reiki master knew they were merely a channel for the attunement energy, not the source.

My final Reiki level to learn was Holy Fire III. I studied this in an online course with William Lee Rand, senior Reiki master/teacher and president of the International Center for Reiki Training. Over three days of class, sixteen students from around the world listened, practiced writing Reiki symbols, and learned prayers to devote ourselves to our work. When we meditated, a beautiful song was played, "Healing Presence" by Julie True. Each afternoon, I signed off from the Zoom room feeling full, a little tired, and grateful to be part of the Reiki community.

For two weeks after the training, I retreated to my altar each evening and practiced Reiki hand positions, body scanning, and self-Reiki. I had also learned to send Reiki to others and practiced this as well.

I wrote an email to Carl telling him how I appreciated all he gave and taught me, his luminosity, his integrity, and his kindness. I wanted to make sure he felt my gratitude for our time together even as we divorced. In harmony with my new work with the Courage Museum, this choice of mine had taken tremendous courage. Each day unfolded in wonder as truth carried me along. I was a living organism of awakenings and revelations that felt like grace.

———

When Covid descended on the world, like most people, I was glued to the news, aghast at the swift movement of the pandemic. I read about the black plague that killed one-third of Europeans between 1347 and 1350, and how law and order had been destroyed. People questioned the government, the church, and political order. It sounded so much like America. Then came the Italian Renaissance in late 14th century, beginning in Florence, which brought political, religious, and artistic change. Renaissance means rebirth, and I claimed that ideal for America and the world.

Confined to my home, I took Zoom courses with the Ananda Meditation School of Meditation and Yoga in the evening and a daytime course on "Awakening Your Intuitive Healing Power" with Dr. Judith Orloff. The intention of the course was to learn to harness our intuition to become vessels for healing. I learned much more about trusting my inner voice, even though I had always had a strong connection to my intuition. I added a weekly online seminar with Natalie Goldberg, "Writing Down the Bones." It was rich with prompts to deepen my writing practice and so good to be in Natalie's presence again.

I missed seeing family. Angelica delivered groceries to my front door—so kind to protect me from going to public places. New York went into lockdown in March 2020, an entire city closed. Stella found out she was pregnant right at that time and moved back to California with her husband, Paul, to be close to me. Although we all got Covid at least once, no one in my immediate family was hospitalized or died, which was like a random miracle, and we mourned with families who had lost loved ones.

We were unable to gather in museums or bookstores, and people even wore masks while hiking and crossed to the other side of the trail or street for protection. In my neighborhood, entire families walked together as schools were closed and workplaces shuttered. It became the land of Zoom.

With less traffic, Los Angeles had blue skies and no exhaust fumes. That part was glorious. Over the next few months, reopenings of many institutions began, and freeways were crowded as people returned to work.

When Covid restrictions were lifted in 2022, life slowly returned to a semblance of normal. In June, I traveled to Washington, DC, for the Smithsonian Folklife Festival. After a two-year hiatus, the festival featured acclaimed musician and arts education advocate Yo-Yo Ma, who performed a concert featuring music and poetry from Afghanistan and beyond. It's title, *The Gifts We Carry: Sounds of Migration and Memory,* was an exemplification of Afghan music through the voicing of poetry, tablas, violins, Yo-Yo Ma's cello, and a rubab, a lute-like stringed instrument. I was a longtime fan of Yo-Yo Ma's artistry, admiring his dedication to traversing continents to plant his art seeds in concert halls, in forests, as well as charming children on Sesame Street. I swooned ever so slightly when introduced to the maestro. After the concert, the skies opened in a wondrous thunderstorm, breaking the humidity and soaking the concert goers.

Lonnie had been installed as the Secretary of the Smithsonian Institution, overseeing the twenty-one museums, National Zoo, and numerous research centers. He had hired Dr. Monique Chism as the Smithsonian's first Under Secretary for Education. I was invited to meet her and sat with her in her office. Her leadership credentials were stellar, and she had studied the performing arts, which I heard in the musicality of her voice. She asked me to join the Education Outreach Working Group. *"Dr. Bunch has directed us to engage pre-K through 12th grade students nationwide through rural initiatives, technology, and paid internships."* Her brown eyes sparkled. *"Your commitment to the Smithsonian will be an asset to our work."*

I was intrigued to serve in another Smithsonian collaboration and answered, *"Yes."*

I had been involved with the Smithsonian for over ten years. It has been a welcoming community for me, and I have made lasting friendships with curators, educators, directors, and staff. They all inspire me to care about the content of information taught in this country, to ensure that America's history is told with integrity, and to remain committed to the mission of disseminating knowledge.

There is a Maori proverb that says, *"Turn your face to the sun and the shadows fall behind you."* I have found so much purpose in every project I have been involved with. There is a presence in life drawing these experiences to me, and I continue to set my sights on the belief that if I continue to seek light, the shadows will fall behind me.

EPILOGUE

THERE IS MUCH MORE IN MY LIFE that has occurred than I have written in these pages—events that brought me to my knees but also achievements and growth that affirmed I am on the right path. This memoir is how I remember moments, holy interactions, the dust from life's gemstones shaken and stirred.

Each element of my existence is bathed in prayer. I acknowledge, trust, and accept the choices that have brought me to deeper understanding of human nature and my own. The phrase: "*Work with integrity, live with compassion*" is a placard on my desk. It is my mantra of intention. I live this more saliently now than I did when I thought I had to compete with others to succeed. My decades of sitting in silence each morning have given me peace with which to look out at the troubled world. Holding sacred beliefs that the work I am doing is guided by my ancestors and matriarchal energies from ancient cultures, I know I can contribute positively to humanity. I am dedicated to work to end racism and discrimination. I value indigeneity as cultural treasure, listening to Elders and following roads to peace. I have been the co-architect of my life with God.

At my desk, with my head down as my fingers paste images onto a collage, or writing in my journal, sitting in my garden, I hear the cry of my animal totem, the red-tailed hawk, reminding me that there is a higher vision that sees all in Divine perspective.

The hawk does not push off with her prey and climb straight into the sky. She ascends gradually with ease and gentleness, circling, tipping her wings, climbing higher and higher.

I, too, have come to this higher place in my life slowly, still able to see the place I recently inhabited, yet enlarging my awareness, and asking for discernment as I continue to seek to be at peace with all things.

My family continues to give me more joy and mercy than I could have ever imagined. Thankfully, my precious Stevie Rio is now flourishing with the sweetest spirit and charm. Stella and her husband, Paul, brought the little wonder, Koa King, into our fold. Stevie and Koa play together, chatting in phrases that tell of innate connections. And Angelica continues her writing and activism with great intelligence and has embarked on creating a free political library.

Mother Teresa of Calcutta said, *"We cannot all do great things, but we can do small things with great love."* Thank you, dear reader, for following my journey. It is a life of great love, compassion, and gratitude, and I wish to meet you on this road of awakening.

HOW TO WALK THROUGH FIRE

As I traversed my journey, here is how I made it through:

- I first acknowledged my life was out of balance with my soul's purpose.

- I sat in silence and prayed for guidance.

- I journaled for twenty minutes—what was out of alignment?

- I created a vision board with images of what I wanted to bring into my life.

- I acknowledged who was toxic to my growth and moved away from them.

- I acknowledged who added light to my life and brought them closer.

- Who will support me and the changes I want to make?

- Now, I was ready to move forward with my new life.

There is a reason, a very special reason, you are here.

Have you leaned in close to a mirror and stared into your eyes? Stood naked in your full-length reflection and smiled? Spread your arms and thrown your head back to the sky? Do you love the strong curve of your back?

It is good to know who you are, without fear, without fences, without the rattle of human striving and misplaced desire. Life brings suffering; the root of survival is courage. Bend with the pain. See the light behind another person's cloud.

Life beats from within. We are voiceless energy from the center of our solar plexus to the crown of our head. Wisdom from Spirit's ageless being thrums in us like an ocean.

You shine.

I shine.

Look into your infinite love.

Live.

Now.

Use this journal on your way:
The Know Yourself Journal by Angelica Santana at artbyjelli.co

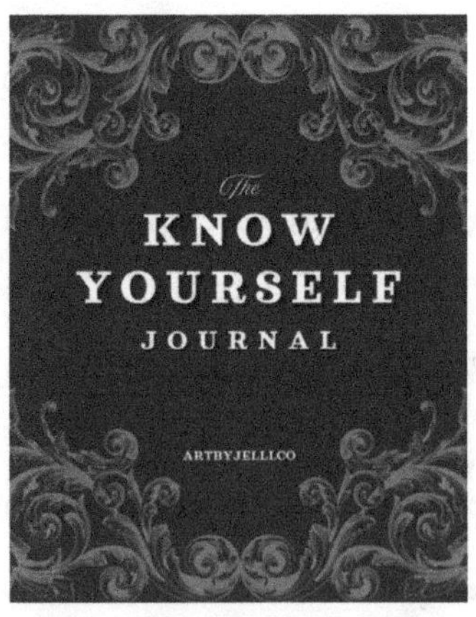

ACKNOWLEDGMENTS

I want to thank the journey I have been blessed to walk. Not everyone comes through life's challenges with inner joy, a sense of wonder, and more love in their hearts, believing that integrity, abundance, and compassion are keys to a good life.

Deepest gratitude to my early readers and encouragers: Beth Benson, Christine Bronstein, Sandra Lucchesi, and Renee Swindle. Beth, your transcription of my journals made my memories more than a tale; you showed me that my writings are talismans.

My editors Jenna Brooks and Shannon Littrell—your guidance and clarity allowed me to reach the finish line. Thank you for shaping the narrative into a cohesive story. I was moved witnessing you see who I was in each layer of my life.

Michael Collopy, your heart of gold brings out the best in my photos. Thank you for serving humanity with humble devotion to justice and peace.

ABOUT THE AUTHOR

DEBORAH SANTANA IS THE AUTHOR of *Space Between the Stars: My Journey to an Open Heart* and the editor of the acclaimed anthology *All the Women in My Family Sing*. Her work has been featured by Vogue, Oprah.com, and NPR, among other national and literary outlets. She is the founder of the Do A Little Foundation, which supports women and girls in the areas of health, education, and happiness. Her work explores identity, social justice, spirituality, and the power of collective voice. She has produced five short documentary films, four with Emmy-award winning director Barbara Rick.

She holds a Master of Arts in Philosophy and Religion with a Concentration in Women's Spirituality. She is a leadership donor of the Smithsonian National Museum of African American History and Culture and a Lead Investor to the Courage Museum in San Francisco.

Willis Women: Virgie (mother), Neoma, Juanita, Ginger, Aggie, Jo Frances

Christ Holy Sanctified Church: early years

Sarah Anasilistine King

Billie Holiday, Willis sisters, and a friend (1947)

Southern Harmony Four: Saunders King,
Eugene Anderson, Alvin Nurse, Willis Barber

S.K. Blues Sheet music

Jo Frances and Saunders King

Bennie Bertram Willis, grandfather

Mom and me

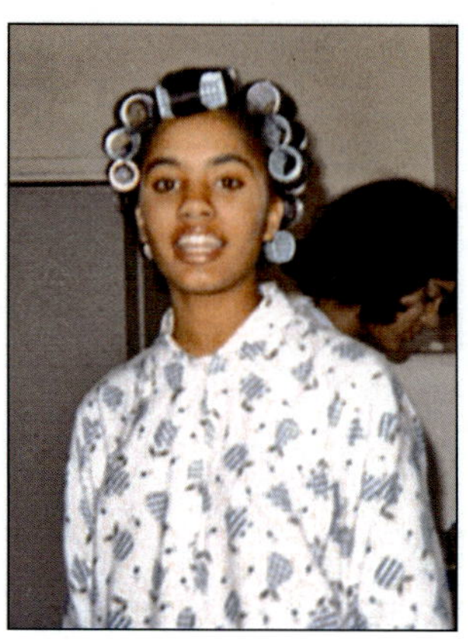

Me in curlers: teenager

Mom and Dad: later years

Deborah at Women's March

His Holiness the Dalai Lama (photo by Michael Collopy)

Salvador opening
Mandela's cell

Nelson Mandela and our family in Johannesburg (2006)
(photo by Barbara Rick)

Green Room in the White House (2016)

Barbara Rick, me, and Jim Anderson

Christmas with Salvador, Angelica, Stella and me
(2024)

Me at Smithsonian

LaTanya Richardson Jackson, me, and Sam Jackson
(photo by Arthur Turner)

CIIS graduation with Stella,
Salvador and Angelica (2015)

Daraja girls and me (2010)

"Do your little bit of good where you are;
it's those little bits of good put together
that overwhelm the world."

ARCHBISHOP DESMOND TUTU

Louisiana
Powell, Arkansas